DATE DUE

COMPREHENSIVE RESEARCH
AND STUDY GUIDE

BLOOM'S

MAJOR
DRAMATISTS

*Tennessee
Williams*

EDITED AND WITH AN
INTRODUCTION BY HAROLD BLOOM

BLOOM'S MAJOR DRAMATISTS

Anton Chekhov
Henrik Ibsen
Arthur Miller
Eugene O'Neill
Shakespeare's Comedies
Shakespeare'sHistories
Shakespeare's Romances
Shakespeare's Tragedies
George Bernard Shaw
Tennessee Williams

BLOOM'S MAJOR NOVELISTS

Jane Austen
The Brontës
Willa Cather
Charles Dickens
William Faulkner
F. Scott Fitzgerald
Nathaniel Hawthorne
Ernest Hemingway
Toni Morrison
John Steinbeck
Mark Twain
Alice Walker

BLOOM'S MAJOR SHORT STORY WRITERS

William Faulkner
F. Scott Fitzgerald
Ernest Hemingway
O. Henry
James Joyce
Herman Melville
Flannery O'Connor
Edgar Allan Poe
J. D. Salinger
John Steinbeck
Mark Twain
Eudora Welty

BLOOM'S MAJOR WORLD POETS

Geoffrey Chaucer
Emily Dickinson
John Donne
T. S. Eliot
Robert Frost
Langston Hughes
John Milton
Edgar Allan Poe
Shakespeare's Poems & Sonnets
Alfred, Lord Tennyson
Walt Whitman
William Wordsworth

BLOOM'S NOTES

The Adventures of Huckleberry Finn
Aeneid
The Age of Innocence
Animal Farm
The Autobiography of Malcolm X
The Awakening
Beloved
Beowulf
Billy Budd, Benito Cereno, & Bartleby the Scrivener
Brave New World
The Catcher in the Rye
Crime and Punishment
The Crucible

Death of a Salesman
A Farewell to Arms
Frankenstein
The Grapes of Wrath
Great Expectations
The Great Gatsby
Gulliver's Travels
Hamlet
Heart of Darkness & The Secret Sharer
Henry IV, Part One
I Know Why the Caged Bird Sings
Iliad
Inferno
Invisible Man
Jane Eyre
Julius Caesar

King Lear
Lord of the Flies
Macbeth
A Midsummer Night's Dream
Moby-Dick
Native Son
Nineteen Eighty-Four
Odyssey
Oedipus Plays
Of Mice and Men
The Old Man and the Sea
Othello
Paradise Lost
The Portrait of a Lady
A Portrait of the Artist as a Young Man

Pride and Prejudice
The Red Badge of Courage
Romeo and Juliet
The Scarlet Letter
Silas Marner
The Sound and the Fury
The Sun Also Rises
A Tale of Two Cities
Tess of the D'Urbervilles
Their Eyes Were Watching God
To Kill a Mockingbird
Uncle Tom's Cabin
Wuthering Heights

COMPREHENSIVE RESEARCH
AND STUDY GUIDE

BLOOM'S
MAJOR
DRAMATISTS

Tennessee
Williams

EDITED AND WITH AN INTRODUCTION
BY HAROLD BLOOM

© 2000 by Chelsea House Publishers, a subsidiary of Haights Cross
Communications.

Introduction © 2000 by Harold Bloom

Printed and bound in the United States of America.

3 5 7 9 8 6 4 2

Library of Congress Cataloging-in-Publication Data

Tennessee Williams / edited and with an introduction by Harold Bloom.
p.   cm.—(Bloom's major dramatists)
Includes bibliographical references and index.
ISBN 0-7910-5240-0
1. Williams, Tennessee, 1911–1983—Examinations and study guides.
I. Bloom, Harold.   II. Series.
PS3545.I5365Z843   1999
812'.54—dc21
99-21422
CIP

Chelsea House Publishers
1974 Sproul Road, Suite 400
Broomall, PA 19008-0914

The Chelsea House World Wide Website address is
http://www.chelseahouse.com

Contributing Editor: Tenley Williams

Contents

User's Guide

This volume is designed to present biographical, critical, and bibliographical information on the playwright's best-known or most important works. Following Harold Bloom's editor's note and introduction are a detailed biography of the author, discussing major life events and important literary accomplishments. A plot summary of each play follows, tracing significant themes, patterns, and motifs in the work.

A selection of critical extracts, derived from previously published material from leading critics, analyzes aspects of each play. The extracts consist of statements from the author, if available, early reviews of the work, and later evaluations up to the present. A bibliography of the author's writings (including a complete list of all works written, cowritten, edited, and translated), a list of additional books and articles on the author and his or her work, and an index of themes and ideas in the author's writings conclude the volume.

~

Harold Bloom is Sterling Professor of the Humanities at Yale University and Henry W. and Albert A. Berg Professor of English at the New York University Graduate School. He is the author of over 20 books and the editor of more than 30 anthologies of literary criticism.

Professor Bloom's works include *Shelley's Mythmaking* (1959), *The Visionary Company* (1961), *Blake's Apocalypse* (1963), *Yeats* (1970), *A Map of Misreading* (1975), *Kabbalah and Criticism* (1975), and *Agon: Toward a Theory of Revisionism* (1982). *The Anxiety of Influence* (1973) sets forth Professor Bloom's provocative theory of the literary relationships between the great writers and their predecessors. His most recent books include *The American Religion* (1992), *The Western Canon* (1994), *Omens of Millennium: The Gnosis of Angels, Dreams, and Resurrection* (1996), and *Shakespeare: The Invention of the Human* (1998), a finalist for the 1998 National Book Award.

Professor Bloom earned his Ph.D. from Yale University in 1955 and has served on the Yale faculty since then. He is a 1985 MacArthur Foundation Award recipient, served as the Charles Eliot Norton Professor of Poetry at Harvard University in 1987–88, and has received honorary degrees from the universities of Rome and Bologna. In 1999, Professor Bloom received the prestigious American Academy of Arts and Letters Gold Medal for Criticism.

Currently, Harold Bloom is the editor of numerous Chelsea House volumes of literary criticism, including the series BLOOM'S NOTES, BLOOM'S MAJOR SHORT STORY WRITERS, BLOOM'S MAJOR POETS, MAJOR LITERARY CHARACTERS, MODERN CRITICAL VIEWS, MODERN CRITICAL INTERPRETATIONS, and WOMEN WRITERS OF ENGLISH AND THEIR WORKS.

Editor's Note

As there are some forty Critical Extracts, I will indicate here only a few that seem to me among the most useful. Thomas F. Van Laan illuminates Catharine's triumphant break-out into the truth in *Suddenly Last Summer*, while Esther Merle Jackson, Ruby Cohn, and C.W.E. Bigsby all find ways of aesthetically defending *The Glass Menagerie*.

A Streetcar Named Desire, Williams' most famous work, receives distinguished commentaries from Joseph N. Riddel and Mary Ann Corrigan, among many other helpful exegetes.

Introduction

HAROLD BLOOM

As a lyrical dramatist, Tennessee Williams manifests the formal influence of Chekhov, yet his principal precursors were the great American lyrical poet, Hart Crane (1899–1932) and the English visionary poet-novelist, D. H. Lawrence (1885–1930). Though his own life span was more substantial (1911–1983) than those of his forerunners, Williams underwent terrible depressions and breakdowns, and the image of Hart Crane's turbulent career emerges frequently in his plays. It is a tribute to Williams's dramatic genius that aspects of Crane vitally inform three of the playwright's very diverse major characters: Tom Wingfield in *The Glass Menagerie*, Blanche DuBois in *A Streetcar Named Desire*, and Sebastian Venable, deceased before *Suddenly Last Summer* opens, yet the central character of the play.

Hart Crane, the most Orphic and self-destructive of all American poets, is of the aesthetic eminence of Walt Whitman, Emily Dickinson, Wallace Stevens, and T. S. Elliot, his own precursors. Williams, perhaps our most gifted dramatist, burned out by his early forties, and in his last three decades produced essentially inadequate work. Ever since I first fell in love with Hart Crane's poetry, almost sixty years ago, I have wondered what the poet of *The Bridge* and "The Broken Tower" would have accomplished, had he not killed himself at thirty-two. One doesn't see Crane burning out; he was poetically strongest at the very end, despite his despair. Williams identified his own art, and his own despair, with Crane's. Tom Wingfield, Blanche Du Bois, and even Sebastian Venable are closer to self-portraits than they are depictions of Hart Crane, but crucial images of Crane's poetry intricately fuse into Williams's visions of himself.

The aesthetic vocation and homosexual identity are difficult to distinguish both in Crane and in Williams, though both poet and playwright develop stratagems, rhetorical and cognitive, that enrich this difficulty without reducing it to case histories. Tom Wingfield's calling will become Williams's, though *The Glass Menagerie* presents Wingfield's quest as a flight away from the family romance, the incestuous images of the mother and the sister. Blanche Du Bois, much closer to Williams himself, risks the playwright's masochistic self-parody, and yet her defeat has considerable aesthetic dignity. More effective on stage than in print, her personality is a touch too wistful to earn the great epitaph from Crane's "The Broken Tower" that Williams insists upon employing:

> And so it was I entered the broken world
> To trace the visionary company of love, its voice
> An instant in the wind (I know not whither hurled)
> But not for long to hold each desperate choice.

One of the oddities of *Suddenly Last Summer* is that Catharine is far closer to an accurate inner portrait of Hart Crane than is the poet Sebastian Venable, who lacks Crane's honesty and courage. Williams's obsession with Crane twists *Suddenly Last Summer* askew, and should not prevent us from seeing that Williams's self-hatred dominates the depiction of Sebastian. For all his gifts, Williams was a far more flawed artist than Crane, whose imaginative heroism was beyond anything Williams could never attain. ❁

Biography of
Tennessee Williams

Tennessee Williams was born Thomas Lanier Williams on March 26, 1911, in Columbus, Mississippi, the second of three children of Cornelius Coffin and Edwina Dakin Williams. His mother had the manners of a Southern gentlewoman; his father, a traveling salesman, preferred whiskey and poker. When Cornelius took an office job with the International Shoe Company, he moved the family to St. Louis. Often, Tom and his older sister Rose would spend time in her small, dark bedroom to play with her prized collection of miniature glass animals. After Tom, Rose, and their younger brother Walter reached adulthood, Cornelius abandoned the family, an event that would become a motif in several of Williams's works, most notably *The Glass Menagerie*.

Rose developed the symptoms of insanity when she was in her teens, and she grew increasingly withdrawn and remote. Edwina would not accept her daughter's illness and tried to force her into a social life, going so far as to enroll her in a secretarial school. Rose was eventually diagnosed as schizophrenic and placed in an asylum. In 1937 she underwent a lobotomy that left her docile and childlike for the rest of her life. Young Tom felt responsible for his sister's mental deterioration. Her symptoms and his awareness of his own homosexuality arose at the same time, and he was never able to separate the events. In all his plays Williams would write about what he knew best: himself and his memories of his family.

In 1927 Williams placed third in a national contest sponsored by the magazine *The Smart Set* for his essay "Can a Good Wife Be a Good Sport?" In 1929 he entered the University of Missouri to study journalism and won an honorable mention for his first play, *Beauty Is the World*. When he flunked ROTC, a training course to prepare him for military service, his father withdrew him from the university. Williams then began work in his father's shoe company, but he became ill and left St. Louis to recuperate at his grandparents' home in Memphis. He returned to enter Washington University in St. Louis, but dropped out and entered the University of Iowa. There, his first full-length plays were produced: *The Fugitive Kind* and *Candles to the Sun* (1936–1937). During this period, culminating in his graduation in 1938, he read widely in world literature and was drawn to playwrights Anton Chekov, Henrik Ibsen, and August Strindberg, English novelist D. H. Lawrence, and American poet Hart Crane.

Williams first used the name "Tennessee Williams" on his short story "The Field of Blue Children," published in *Story* magazine in 1939. The same year he traveled, received a $1,000 Rockefeller grant, and began a full-length play, *Battle of Angels*. In 1940 he moved to New York City and enrolled in an advanced playrighting seminar taught by John Gassner at The New School. From 1941 through 1943 he worked at various odd jobs, as well as for MGM studio as a screenwriter, before becoming a full-time writer in 1944. His first published play was *At Liberty*, appearing in *American Scenes*, edited by Williams Kozlenko (1941). *The Glass Menagerie*, whose family of lonely, slowly disintegrating people mirrors Williams's own childhood, was his first major success. *Menagerie* was produced in Chicago on December 26, 1945, and won the New York Critics' Circle Award, the first of four Williams would receive. *A Streetcar Named Desire* (1947) solidified his status as a major American playwright and won Williams the first of two Pulitzer Prizes. *Summer and Smoke* (1947), won him a second New York Critics' Circle Award. *The Rose Tattoo*, produced in 1951, won a Tony Award; the same year the film version of *Streetcar* was released. *Cat on a Hot Tin Roof* (1955) won for Williams a third New York Critics' Circle Award and a second Pulitzer Prize; the film version of the play was released in 1958. *Orpheus Descending* (a rewrite of Williams's unsuccessful early play *Battle of Angels*) opened in New York in 1957, followed by *Garden District* (consisting of the plays *Something Unspoken* and *Suddenly Last Summer*) off-Broadway, in 1958, *Sweet Bird of Youth* (1959), *Period of Adjustment* (1960), *The Night of the Iguana* (1961), and a one-act version of *The Milk Train Doesn't Stop Here Anymore*, which was presented at the Festival of Two Worlds in Spoleto, Italy.

Tennessee Williams was one of the most popularly successful and most critically lauded and vilified dramatists of the twentieth century. His treatment of the theme of homosexuality in his works has been both admired for its audacity and disparaged for its ambiguity. His plays are largely noted for their moving portrayal of people living in deteriorating circumstances, often surrounded by madness and violence. Williams has been criticized for overindulging in sexuality and violence, and his later, rather disjointed and stylized plays have been subjected to particularly harsh criticism. Nonetheless, among Williams's more than seventy produced plays are some of the most significant dramas of modern times. Though all his work is controversial, and much of it is considered insignificant, few would question Williams's immense influence and position as one of America's preeminent dramatists. He is author of twenty-five full-length plays, dozens of short plays and screenplays, two novels, *The Roman Spring of Mrs. Stone* (1950) and *Moise and the World of Reason* (1975), a novella, three books of poetry, and several collections of short stories, many of which served as kernels for later plays. *Memoirs* was published in 1975, and *Where I Live: Selected Essays* in 1978. His last plays were produced in 1981: *A House Not Meant to Stand,* in Chicago, and *Something Cloudy Something Clear,* in New York. His works have been translated into twenty-seven languages. Williams received an honorary degree from Harvard University in 1982.

Williams began psychoanalysis in 1956, the year his father died, and, in 1963, suffered a prolonged period of depression after the death of his lover, Frank Merlo, of lung cancer. Williams had met and fallen in love with Merlo in 1947, while living in New Orleans. The two traveled together to Italy where Williams prepared to write *The Rose Tattoo,* a work that, in many ways, tells the story of his meeting Merlo. It is the only of his major plays to have a happy ending. He continued to write prolifically, though his works were no longer well received by critics. Upon the death of Merlo, Williams entered a ten-year depression that he would refer to as his "stoned age." He converted to Roman Catholicism in 1969 and, the same year, was hospitalized for three months after a nervous collapse. Bizarrely choking on a plastic bottlecap while under the influence of barbiturates, Tennessee Williams died on February 24, 1983, in New York City. He is buried in St. Louis, Missouri. ❀

Plot Summary of
Suddenly Last Summer

Critical views on *Suddenly Last Summer* are divided: some feel that the play marks the peak of Williams's playrighting skills, while others feel it indicates the beginning of his artistic decline. However, most agree that this work, which is set in New Orleans, is one of Williams's most autobiographical plays. *Suddenly Last Summer* is a long, one-act play with four scenes. The work is constructed as two monologues, the first developing the scene for the story told in the second. The events of central character Sebastian Venable's story are never put into action on the stage but are told by his young cousin, Catharine. The play focuses on the effects of these unseen events involving Sebastian upon the lives of the characters: both by Catharine's telling of the events and Violet Venable's attempt to silence the story.

The story's Gothic-style treatment of evil begins in **scene one** with Mrs. Violet Venable, a wealthy Southern dowager, who describes her relationship with her beloved son, Sebastian, who is now dead. An adoring, overprotective mother, she had always accompanied him on long, summer travels that culminated in his writing an annual "Poem of Summer." She describes Sebastian as a sensitive poet, but we will learn that, in reality, he was a monstrous and manipulative man. One year Violet had suffered a stroke and, because she had been unable to travel, Sebastian had invited his young cousin, Catharine, to accompany him. She witnessed his brutal death and the trauma has left her near hysteria, but coherent enough to suggest that Sebastian had been in some way responsible for the horror of his own death: His homosexual advances upon a group of young boys led to his being devoured by them. Mrs. Venable is determined to preserve her idealized memory of her son, to suppress by any means the truth that Catharine struggles to articulate.

Catharine is confined by her aunt to a mental asylum, "babbling" the strange story about Sebastian's death at Cabeza de Lobo in the Encantadas (the Galápagos Islands). The girl has been released into her aunt's care but suffers from horrific nightmares and is given to sudden, uncontrolled outbursts of violent behavior. Mrs. Venable engages a neurosurgeon, Dr. Cukrowicz, an expert on lobotomy, to quite literally cut the story out of Catharine's brain. (The doctor's

Polish name, we are told, means "sugar" and, ironically, the doctor does not so sweeten Mrs. Venable's life.) She promises the doctor that she will fund a neurosurgery wing to the hospital in her son's name if he will agree to operate on her niece.

Both Sebastian and Catharine are often seen as emblems of social and personal conflict, which are distinctive as recurring themes in Williams's works: Donald P. Costello writes "the world will not face Catharine's clear view of the cannibalistic nature of man on the earth—'the true story of our time and the world we live in.' So the world makes Catharine into a fugitive: she is put into an asylum; she is threatened with a lobotomy; she, instead of society, is made the one who is 'perverse.'" Sebastian, Arthur Ganz tells us, is "the homosexual so often for [Williams] the symbol of the lonely, rejected exile—[who] becomes the rejector, the sinner who must be punished." Sebastian is revealed by Williams to have been an ego-centric and sadistic personality who used his mother and his cousin to attract male companions. Sebastian became food for the savage boys of Cabeza de Lobo much like the turtles that were devoured by the carnivorous birds of the Encantadas. In Williams's moral scheme Sebastian is punished primarily because he is a homo-sexual, but the theme of corruption is more universal: As Ganz notes, Sebastian hated rather than loved "his suffering fellow crea-tures," and "feeding upon people like one of the devouring birds of the Encantadas. . . . [he could not] escape corruption and despair."

Williams structures the play as a battle between Mrs. Venable and Catharine. Though weakened by the stroke, Violet is a formidable adversary. In the **second scene** Catharine and Sister Felicity, Catharine's guardian from the asylum, are introduced. Though Sister Felicity is a minor character, her silent witness to the events seems to mirror our own. Dr. Cukrowicz notices that Catharine is not the lunatic her aunt had described. In the **third scene** Catharine's mother and brother appear, desperate to claim money from Sebastian's estate and unmoved by Catharine's suffering. The **fourth scene** focuses upon Catharine and her climactic description of Sebastian's death. She also describes her involvement with a married man, a confidence she had shared with Sebastian who had then invited her to accom-pany him on his summer trip. Using injections of sodium pen-tathol, Dr. Cukrowicz discovers that Catharine's story is true, and he confronts Mrs. Venable with the truth about her son's death. ❁

List of Characters in
Suddenly Last Summer

Mrs. Violet Venable is a very wealthy Southern dowager. She commits her young niece, Catharine, to a mental asylum and wants to have the girl lobotomized in order to protect the idealized memory she keeps of her dead son Sebastian. Because she had suffered a stroke she was unable to accompany her son on their annual summer trip. She describes Sebastian as a sensitive poet.

Catharine is Violet's niece and Sebastian's cousin. She accompanies Sebastian and is traumatized by his savage death at the hands of a group of young native boys whom he has apparently engaged in homosexual acts. She tells and retells the horrific details of the murder and, in order to silence her, Mrs. Venable has her committed to a mental asylum, then seeks to have her lobotomized. Her qualities of mercy and goodness contrast Sebastian's corruption.

Dr. Cukrowicz is a neurosurgeon whom Mrs. Venable engages to treat her niece for what she maintains are psychotic delusions about Sebastian's death. She promises him that she will fund a neurosurgery wing in her son's name if, in exchange, he will lobotomize Catharine. In the process of evaluating Catharine's mental condition he discovers that her story is true, and he confronts Mrs. Venable about her own responsibility in her son's death.

Sebastian, although dead before the play begins, is the foundation of the play. He is hedonistic, amoral, and homosexual, a sign of our cultural and moral corruption. He makes his mother and his cousin complicit in his seductions of young men and, in the final case, young boys. He is literally devoured by a group of island boys, an event Catharine describes in horrific detail. ❀

Critical Views of
Suddenly Last Summer

ARTHUR GANZ ON THE HOMOSEXUAL AS EXILE

[Arthur Ganz is the author of *Pinter, a Collection of Critical Essays, Realms of the Self: Variations on a Theme in Modern Drama,* and a critical volume on the works of George Bernard Shaw. In this excerpt Ganz discusses Sebastian's corruption, despair, and symbolic martyrdom.]

In *Suddenly Last Summer,* the last play of what may be called the "punishment" group, Williams has produced a work in which the homosexual—so often for him the symbol of the lonely, rejected exile—becomes the rejector, the sinner who must be punished.

But neither this shift in Williams' usual pattern nor the *bizarrerie* of the play's atmosphere should conceal the fact that *Suddenly Last Summer* follows closely the structure of the other plays in this group. Once more the pivotal figure, the exile homosexual, has met a violent death before the opening of the play. As the sterile Brick is contrasted with Big Daddy, the life-giving father of *Cat,* so the cruel Sebastian is played off against the loving and merciful Catharine who gives herself not, it seems, out of desire but as an act of rescue. "We walked through the wet grass to the great misty oaks," she says, "as if somebody was calling us for help there." If we remember that this act of rescue is exactly what Blanche, Alma and Brick failed to perform, we realize that Williams means us to accept Catharine as entirely good. Although Sebastian is, as we expect him to be, the loveless rejector who is punished for his sins, there is a surprising similarity between his vision of a world dominated by remorseless cruelty—as expressed in the description of the Encantadas, the Galápagos Islands, where baby sea turtles are killed and devoured by carnivorous birds of prey—and the vision of a world undergoing perpetual punishment expressed in "Desire and the Black Masseur." However, in punishing Sebastian, Williams is not disclaiming this vision. Sebastian's sin lay not in perceiving the world as, for Williams, it is, but in his believing, with a pride bordering on *hubris,* that he could exalt himself above his kind, that he could feed upon people like one of the devouring birds of the Encantadas. As always in

Williams, the punishment monstrously fits the crime. As Sebastian had cruelly watched the turtles being eaten, as he had fed the fruit flies to the devouring plant, so he is fed to the band of children whom he has perverted and is devoured by them.

Sebastian's crime then is the very one committed by Blanche, Alma and Brick. He has turned away from his suffering fellow creatures and, instead of offering love, has offered hate. He has not understood, as Catharine has, that although all men may be on a stricken ship sinking into the sea, "that's no reason for everyone drowning for hating everyone drowning." And yet there is a difficulty for the spectator in accepting the nature of Sebastian's punishment, however fierce he knows Williams' morality to be. It is not merely that Sebastian's fate is so violently grotesque but that, unlike Blanche and Brick, he has not performed a specific act that brings his punishment upon him; he is punished for what he is rather than for what he does. He is not only a rejector but also a homosexual, always in Williams' work an object simultaneously of sympathy and of revulsion. The ambiguity ⟨. . .⟩ appears in all Williams plays that touch on homosexuality. There is an intimate connection between the guilty rejector and the martyred homosexual; the punishment visited on the former regularly echoes the fate of the latter, so that the two characters are not always distinguishable. In *Streetcar* the rejector and the homosexual victim were separate, but both met desperate ends. In the ambiguous Brick these figures began to converge, and in *Suddenly Last Summer* they have completely coalesced. The pain felt by the cruel rejector is also felt by the sterile and guilty homosexual; neither can escape corruption and despair.

Here lies the source of that vision of universal corruption that pervades so much of Williams' work and that makes it at once so violent and so pathetic. In a world dominated by cruelty, Williams maintains, the innocent are not only destroyed; eventually, they too are corrupted.

—Arthur Ganz, "The Desperate Morality of the Plays of Tennessee Williams," *American Scholar* (Spring 1962): 278–294. Reprinted in *The Chelsea House Library of Literary Criticism: Twentieth-Century American Literature*, vol. 7, ed. Harold Bloom (New York: Chelsea House Publishers, 1988): 4323–4324.

GILBERT DEBUSSCHER ON SEBASTIAN VENABLE AND THE DEATH OF A SAINT

[Gilbert Debusscher teaches English and American litera-ture at the University of Brussels, Belgium. He is the author of *Jonson and Elizabethan Comedy: Essays in Dramatic Rhetoric, Edward Albee: Tradition and Renewal,* and numerous articles on American theater. In this extract Debusscher notes the identification of Sebastian Venable with the life and the death of his patron saint.]

We thus get an indication that early in his career Williams was aware of the possibility of prolonging the meaning of his charac-ters and of making his particulars resonate with broader overtones. That he did not pursue the device further in this particular instance is probably due to his tyro's inability to control his referential method properly, an inability which manifests itself in the confusing tangle of Christian and mythical echoes that reverberate through this first full-length play.

Eighteen years and seven plays later, in *Suddenly Last Summer* (1958), Williams appears in full command of his craft and in this instance the indications of partial identification of Sebastian Venable with his patron saint are more systematic and varied.

As in the earlier example, it is a seemingly incidental mention in Catharine Holly's report that brings the figure of St. Sebastian into the picture. Says Catharine:

> "In Cabeza de Lobo there is a beach that's named for Sebastian's name saint, it's known as La Playa San Sebastian, and that's where we started spending all afternoon, every day."

Williams' familiarity with the circumstances of the martyr's legend is evidenced in a 1948 poem titled "San Sebastiano de Sodoma." The playwright is obviously aware that St. Sebastian was a Roman martyr traditionally considered the lover of Emperor Diocletian (Williams refers to him in the poem as "an emperor's concubine"). After bitterly reproaching him with his conversion to Christianity, the Emperor is reported to have "delivered him over to certain archers of Mauritania to be shot to death" because of his new faith. The handsome youth survived and was nursed back to health by a pious widow. After recovering from his wounds, Sebastian returned to Diocletian to plead the cause of the Christians. "Recovering from his surprise, he (the emperor) gave orders for him to be seized and beaten to death with cudgels and his body thrown into the common sewer." This time Sebastian dies and again a woman appears but now to bury him.

The critics have been prompt to trace the references to the saint's legend in Williams' play. Sebastian Venable possesses the good looks generally attributed to his patron saint. In this connection, William E. Taylor quotes the *Encyclopedia Britannica* according to which "St. Sebastian is a favorite subject of sacred art, being most generally represented undraped, and severely though not mortally wounded with arrows." It is interesting to note that a French erotologist, Raymond De Becker, would comment that the representation of St. Sebastian pierced with arrows, i.e. the scene of his life made famous through the plastic arts, is the "sujet privilégié des peintres homoérotiques de la Chrétienté." Williams suggests an unmistakable homosexual reference in the title of his poem "San Sebastiano de Sodoma" and makes his Sebastian character also into a homosexual.

The stories of the two characters also present important points of contact. Both heroes are connected with two women. They are represented in the modern version by Mrs. Venable and Catharine. The first helps Sebastian survive a particularly painful experience: the "pious widow" nurses the Roman character back to life after the torture by the archers; Mrs. Venable tears her son away from the Buddhist monks. The second contributes to celebrating the last rites for the dead: the Roman matron buries the saint's bodily remains; the American girl figuratively inters her cousin's usurped reputation. Even more immediately reminiscent of the saint's legend are the circumstances of Sebastian's death. As the Japanese critic Tatsumi Funatsu pointed out, the description by Catharine of Sebastian's assailants is carefully worded so as to remind us of the arrows with which St. Sebastian is almost struck to death:

> "There were naked children along the beach, a band of frightfully thin and dark naked children that look like a flock of plucked birds, and they would come *darting up* (. . .) Sebastian started to run and they all screamed at once and seemed to *fly in the air* (. . .)"

The context of the play allows us to endow the arrow with sexual symbolism and thus to view the young phallus bearers who pursue Sebastian up the mountain as corresponding to the instruments of torture of the legend.

—Gilbert Debusscher, "Tennessee Williams' Lives of the Saints: A Playwright's Obliquity" (editor's title), *Revue des Langues Vivantes* 40 (1974): 449–456. Reprinted in *Tennessee Williams: A Collection of Critical Essays*, ed. Stephen S. Stanton (Englewood Cliffs, N.J: Prentice-Hall, 1977): 150–152.

ESTHER MERLE JACKSON ON THE ANTI-HERO

[In this extract Esther Merle Jackson notes that some of Williams's characters are not traditional examples of mankind but creatures caught in destructive life processes.]

One of the most controversial aspects of the drama of Tennessee Williams is his use of an anti-heroic protagonist as an image of man. Williams appears to reject the Aristotelian concept of the protagonist and to substitute for it an anti-hero, the personification of a humanity neither good, knowledgeable, nor courageous. In Blanche, Alma, Brick, Kilroy, Val, Chance, and Shannon, we see this anti-heroic image of man. Even those figures who command some sympathy, characters such as Tom in *The Glass Menagerie* and Catharine—the victim of *Suddenly Last Summer*—may be described . . . as "non-beings." . . . Williams claims that such is the image of modern man—poised as he is between the contrary imperatives of his world. As he examines humanity through the patched glass of his synthetic myth, the playwright perceives a creature transfixed in a moment of stasis, halted at the point of transition in the process of becoming. . . .

Although contemporary dramatists accept certain aspects of the ethics of Aristotle, they do not feel that his definition of the hero is in every sense an accurate description of a virtuous man in the twentieth century. Arthur Miller, for example, points out that many aspects of Aristotle's system of ethics are today obsolete.

The image of man in the twentieth century, writes Miller, must be rooted in an open system of values appropriate to a democratic society. Tennessee Williams writes that the most pressing moral problem of man in the twentieth century is to avoid extinction: "to beat the game of being against non-being." The crux of the argument which has led to the modification of the Aristotelian hero lies in changes in the perception of experience, in the accumulation of new knowledges about and new hopes for the human species.

One of the most dramatic of the changes which have affected the idea of the hero is that embodied in the science of psychology, for classic ideals of "goodness," "nobility," and "courage" have, under psychological scrutiny, assumed a significantly different aspect. Equally affecting, perhaps, has been the political history of modern Europe: a record of suffering, wars, and conflicts which have exacted a tremendous physical, spiritual, and psychological toll. Because of a new sense of historical crisis, the hero, a man of action, has grown less appealing as an image of present moral and ethical aspirations than the anti-hero, a man of reflection and contemplation. But perhaps an even more profound change in perspective is represented in the growing influence of the Judaeo-Christian ethic on the moral aspirations of the common man. Despite the apparent record of history, the principles of Christianity have become, in the past century, a more meaningful part of a common standard for human action. The substitution of the "inner-oriented" ethic of the Christian protagonist for the "outer-directed" heroism of the Greek hero is one of the significant contemporary adjustments in Western drama. It is this change which has materially altered the idea of tragic action and which has produced a new concept of dramatic character.

In a discussion of contemporary form, René-Marill Albérès describes the contemporary anti-hero as a "theological protagonist." He is an image of man seeking to know the universe, to define its purpose, and to discover his ultimate meaning in its pattern. Albérès describes the contemporary motive in these words: "The contemporary theatre, like the novel, becomes a research and a quest. It makes itself idealistic, its characters force themselves toward that which they can never find." For Albérès the anti-heroic quest is a journey toward moral commitment. Williams seems to confirm this judgment in his play *The Night of the Iguana*; he gives in this work the account of a heretic, the story of the world-weary priest Shannon who searches the earth for the face of God. Shannon follows the moral progression described by St. John of the Cross as the "dark night of the soul." He proceeds in contrary motion, in flight from the presence of God; but, like St. John, he finds that the "way down" leads up. Shannon declares that his search has brought him finally to that presence which he has sought:

> Yes, I see him, I hear him, I know him. And if he doesn't know that I know him, let him strike me dead with a bolt of his lightning.

Williams' construction of his anti-heroic protagonist, his "negative saint," is based on a radical perception of new dangers for mankind, as well as on the recognition of new modes of courage. What are these dangers? In *A Streetcar Named Desire* the playwright cautions the spectator against societal regression, against the capitulation of humanity to the laws of the jungle. In later plays—*Cat on a Hot Tin Roof, Camino Real, Suddenly Last Summer, Sweet Bird of Youth*, and *The Night of the Iguana*—he warns against the moral and spiritual disintegration of mankind. To interpret present dimensions of the human dilemma, Williams creates a protagonist who is conceived in anti-traditional terms. Brick, Kilroy, Catharine, Chance, and Shannon are not "mankind" in the sense of classic, neoclassic, romantic, or realistic definitions. They are images of a humanity diminished by time and history. They are each characterized by an inner division, by a fragmentation so complete that it has reduced them to partialities. They are "un-beings," caught in the destructive life-process.

—Esther Merle Jackson, "The Anti-Hero in the Plays of Tennessee Williams" (editor's title), in *The Broken World of Tennessee Williams* (Madison: University of Wisconsin Press, 1965). Reprinted in *Tennessee Williams: A Collection of Critical Essays*, ed. Stephen S. Stanton (Englewood Cliffs, N.J: Prentice-Hall, 1977): 87–89.

LOUISE BLACKWELL ON WOMEN AND THE ELUSIVE "RIGHT" MATE

[Louise Blackwell is co-editor of a critical volume on the works of Lillian Smith. In this excerpt Blackwell discusses the psychological needs that motivate Blanche DuBois, Laura Wingfield, Stella Kowalski, and Mrs. Venable and Catharine.]

In a dozen plays written between 1945 and 1961, Tennessee Williams chose to feature women as major characters more often than men. This choice, in view of his unusual perception, has enabled him to display his talent in a remarkable succession of plays. After 1961, as Williams' doubts and fears about his own artistic powers have grown, his faith in sexual adjustment as the key to the meaning of life has waned; none of his more recent females attain happiness through lasting sexual relationships; some are not even concerned with such happiness; all suffer from physical or emotional mutilation (or both). For them, communication with another person in itself becomes more difficult and unattainable, or their restless search for a mate goes on without hope of fulfillment. Because of this shift in theme and characterization in the later plays, they have not been included in this short study.

Early in his career, the subtlety of Williams' themes and characterizations resulted in misinterpretation on the part of critics and audiences. From *A Streetcar Named Desire* (1947) through *The Night of the Iguana* (1961), however, Williams made his themes explicit by having major characters discuss them, but his purpose continued to be lost on some viewers and readers. As late as 1961, for instance, Hodding Carter wrote in the *New York Times Magazine* that he did not recognize the "Southern womenfolk" portrayed by Williams. On the other hand, Signi Lenea Falk has called the playwright's female characters either Southern gentlewomen or Southern wenches. While it is true that many of Williams' characters speak with Southern accents, close scrutiny reveals that their problems are the old, universal ones of the human heart in its search for reality and meaning in life. ⟨. . .⟩

Williams is making a commentary on Western culture by dramatizing his belief that men and women find reality and meaning in life through satisfactory sexual relationships. His drama derives from the characters' recognition of certain needs within themselves and their consequent demands for the "right" mate. Frustration is the surface evidence of the predicament of his female characters, but Williams is careful to distinguish the underlying reasons for their behavior. ⟨. . .⟩

One approach to the study of these characters is to categorize them according to their situation at the time of the action, so long as we allow for variations within each category. Thus:

1. *Women who have learned to be maladjusted through adjustment to abnormal family relationships and who strive to break through their bondage in order to find a mate.* ⟨. . .⟩

Blanche DuBois of *A Streetcar Named Desire* (1947) was a dutiful child, remaining with her aged parents long beyond the marrying age for most women and later staying behind to try to save the family estate, while her sister, Stella, went out to find her place in the world. Since Blanche had adjusted to an abnormal family life, she was unable, when she had the opportunity, to relate to the so-called normal world of her sister. She was, in fact, following a family pattern when she became sexually profligate after the death of her parents. In a discussion of property matters, she says that the plantation was disposed of gradually by "improvident grandfathers and father and uncles and brothers" who exchanged the land for their "epic fornications."

In an earlier play, *The Glass Menagerie* (1945), Laura Wingfield has learned to be maladjusted from her mother, Amanda. In his notes on the characters, Williams states that Amanda Wingfield is "a little woman of great but confused vitality, clinging frantically to another time and place. . . . She is not paranoiac, but her life is paranoia." Amanda's husband and son have long since deserted her, but Laura, who has been crippled since birth, has no escape open to her. She must adjust to her mother who is so unrealistic that she denies that Laura is crippled. According to the author, she has "failed to establish contact with reality, continues to live vitally in her illusions." Indeed, the only way Laura can survive is to retreat into her own delusions. ⟨. . .⟩

2. *Women who have subordinated themselves to a domineering and often inferior person in an effort to attain reality and meaning through communication with another person.*

Stella Kowalski, in *A Streetcar Named Desire* (1947), is superior in background and personal endowments to her mate, but she subordinates herself to his way of life because they have a satisfying sexual relationship. When her sister Blanche cannot believe that Stella is happy with her crude husband, Stella tells her that "there are things that happen between a man and a woman in the dark—that sort of make everything else seem—unimportant." When Stella is willing to send her sister to a mental institution rather than believe that Stanley has raped Blanche we see just how far a seemingly gentle and attractive woman will go to defend her sexual partner. ⟨. . .⟩

3. *Women who struggle to make relationships with men who are unable or unwilling to make lasting relationships.*

In four plays, *Cat on a Hot Tin Roof* (1955), *Orpheus Descending* (1957), *Suddenly Last Summer* (1958), and *Period of Adjustment* (1960). Williams created a group of women who are remarkable for their sexual demands upon men who are either homosexual or otherwise inadequate to make a lasting relationship. ⟨. . .⟩

In *Suddenly Last Summer*, Mrs. Venable and Catharine clash over a dead man, Sebastian. Sebastian was Mrs. Venable's son and Catharine her niece. Throughout his life Sebastian, a would-be poet and sexual misfit, was pampered, overprotected, and dominated by his mother. Catharine was in love with Sebastian and, at the request of his mother, she willingly agreed to travel abroad with him. Later, in spite of the threats of Mrs. Venable, she insisted upon telling the truth about how Sebastian was killed and partly devoured by a group of cannibalistic boys on a tropical island. The unique thing about Catharine is that she yearned for a sexual relationship with a man, her cousin, whom she knew to be weak and strangely perverted.

—Louise Blackwell, *South Atlantic Bulletin* 35 (March 1970): 9–14. Revised version reprinted in *Tennessee Williams: A Collection of Critical Essays*, ed. Stephen S. Stanton (Englewood Cliffs, N.J: Prentice-Hall, 1977): 100–105.

THOMAS F. VAN LAAN ON CATHARINE'S TRIUMPH OF VOICE

[Thomas F. Van Laan is former Chairman of the English Department at Rutgers University. His interests range from the Elizabethan dramatists to the moderns. In this excerpt Van Laan points out the irony that, in order for Catharine to be silenced, Mrs. Venable must allow her first to be heard.]

Suddenly Last Summer is gaining increasing recognition as one of Williams' best plays because we are finally discovering how it is shaped and what it is about. Contrary to much that has been written, it is not a study of Sebastian Venable, sensationalistic or otherwise; rather, it dramatizes a conflict between opposing versions (or visions) of Sebastian, and especially a conflict for supremacy between the two who hold them. Catharine Holly eventually emerges as the protagonist of the play, but Mrs. Venable is the one who sets its action in motion. She seeks to silence Catharine in order to prevent her from voicing a version of her son which she cannot bear to have heard. Mrs. Venable's motive allies her with Williams' victims, who try to shut up the voice of hostile reality, but what the playwright stresses in his portrait of her is the vicious and malicious relentlessness with which she pursues her goal. As a result, *Suddenly Last Summer* joins *A Streetcar Named Desire*, *Orpheus Descending*, and *Sweet Bird of Youth* in the starkness with which it dramatizes the clash between aggressor and victim; at the same time, it is Williams' purest and most striking version of the motif of one character's attempts to shut up another. ⟨. . .⟩

   Mrs. Venable's intentions and her determination are inescapably clear, and it seems that she is likely to have her way, for she has wealth and power, she is practiced in the successful application of these assets, and she has a promising ally in Dr. Cukrowicz, who needs her financial assistance. And yet this first section of the play also contains a number of touches that undercut Mrs. Venable and thus cast doubt on her ultimate triumph. She has scarcely begun her monologue before momentarily breaking it off to acknowledge that "I've already talked myself breathless and dizzy." She vows that it's not she but Catharine who will "collapse" in their struggle, and yet a few minutes later she is on the point of *physical* collapse as she "*staggers*" and must be assisted to a chair by the Doctor. Constantly, as she presents her version of Sebastian, she introduces various criticisms of her son and their behavior together, and, while her purpose is to refute them, one result is that they manage to get expressed. All these details call her intention and her talk—*her* version of Sebastian—into question. But the most telling point against her in this opening section of the play is the irony that in order to show the doctor why Catharine must be silenced she is providing the opportunity for Catharine's version of Sebastian to be heard. ⟨. . .⟩

Even more important than the defeat of Mrs. Venable for establishing Catharine's triumph in the struggle is the staging of her narration. After Mrs. Venable agrees to be silent, the ensuing moments, like the beginning of the play, constitute a virtual monologue. As Catharine's speeches become longer and longer, the only other voice to be heard is that of the Doctor, who gives her encouragement and reinforces by echo many of the details of her account. Moreover, "*the light gradually changes as the girl gets deeper into her story: the light concentrates on Catharine, the other figures sink into shadow,*" and "*During the monologue the lights have changed, the surrounding area has dimmed out and a hot white spot is focused on Catharine.*" At the beginning of the play, Mrs. Venable had tried to possess it, to transform it from drama into a monologue of *her* making; at the end Catharine, without trying, succeeds. As the staging suggests, the play and Catharine in monologue have become virtually identical—so much so, in fact, that many have been misled into finding the drama of the occasion in the story Catharine relates rather than in her act of relating it.

Catharine's triumph over Mrs. Venable, in its basic outline, is like that of Brick over Big Daddy at the end of Act Two of *Cat on a Hot Tin Roof*. However, by deflecting the role of explicit silencer from Catharine to the Doctor and by keeping Catharine's motives free of any trace of vindictiveness, Williams breaks the pattern of the former play in which the victim, pushed too far, in his efforts to silence the aggressor becomes an aggressor himself. Part of Catharine's triumph is her remaining free from this trap. Mrs. Venable's initial sense of herself as victim is erased in the emphasis on the truth of Catharine's account and the necessity of its being spoken. Mrs. Venable thus keeps the role of aggressor, as her final action affirms, and in this case the aggressor is clearly and completely routed. The ending of the play does not, however, leave this triumph untouched by complicating ambiguity. Catharine gets to speak out, to accomplish what the aggressor has striven to prevent, but the truth she tells—of how Sebastian was torn to pieces by the children—fits all too comfortably into the vision of the world that Sebastian held and that he thought he saw confirmed by the destruction of the baby turtles on the Galapagos Islands. It is the same vision, moreover, which Mrs. Venable has tried to fulfill in her treatment of Catharine Holly. Thus Catharine's triumph over her aggressor ironically enables Williams to provide one of the most hideous versions in all of his plays of the usual outcome of the aggressor-victim pattern.

The motif I have been examining is not central to Williams' other powerful full-length pre-1960 plays: *A Streetcar Named Desire, Orpheus Descending,* and *Sweet Bird of Youth.* But it is perhaps implicit in them, for they all end with the aggressors permanently shutting up their victims, literally so in *Streetcar,* where Blanche, her story not believed and on her way to the state mental institution, in effect suffers the fate Mrs. Venable intended for Catharine Holly. These other plays also imply the motif in that their protagonist-victims all possess some touch of the poet. For what Williams is doing in this motif is translating his dark vision of human interaction and of human existence in a hostile universe into the terms of his occupation—or, better, his calling—as writer. This is most evident in *The Glass Menagerie,* which is defined as a play by Tom—his ambiguous triumph over Amanda's efforts to silence him—and in *Suddenly Last Summer,* in which Catharine Holly uses story, parable, and vision—the products of a writer— to witness to the truth. Those who strive to speak in *Cat on a Hot Tin Roof* are not seen as artists in the same symbolic way, but their efforts add another implication to the resonance of the motif by identifying the ultimate aggressor as Death.

In Williams' vision, the writer is engaged in a constant battle to give himself life through words. Sometimes he seeks to record the truth of reality; sometimes he seeks to create a more desirable alternative; but in any case he keeps producing words, waging his conflict with a world that would prefer to shut him up because his words, in either form, are threatening, and, for a while at least, keeping Death at bay. The plays I have examined show us that we are all in some sense writers, using our words to express ourselves and our realities, and they show us what those of us who actually are writers can do for us. Surprisingly, given the essential darkness of Williams' vision, they also show us the genuine possibility of triumph in the struggle. In *Suddenly Last Summer*, for example, although one representative of the writer—Sebastian—suffers the feared result of the aggressor-victim conflict, he is given renewed life through another representative's truthful account of him, and in her triumph Williams manages to save in art the sister whom he could not save in life. Of the three plays I have examined, the darkest is the first and supposedly most gentle of the three; in the others there is some kind of ultimate triumph through words, however muted that triumph may be by ambiguity. This—aside from the fact that he had to—perhaps explains why Williams himself (despite the ever obsessive pursuit of sex, the alcohol, the drugs, the paranoia, the mental breakdowns, the declining imaginative powers, and the recurring failures) kept producing his words right up to the very end.

—Thomas F. Van Laan, "'Shut Up!' 'Be Quiet!' 'Hush!' Talk and Its Suppression in Three Plays by Tennessee Williams," *Comparative Drama* 22, no. 3 (Fall 1988): 257–263.

JOHN M. CLUM ON THE HOMOSEXUAL ARTIST EXPOSED

[John M. Clum is Professor of English and Theatre at Duke University. He is the author of *Staging Gay Lives: An Anthology of Contemporary Gay Theater, Displacing Homophobia*, and volumes on the works of Paddy Chayefsky and Ridgely Torence. In this excerpt Clum discusses the danger to truth, for Sebastian and for Brick, when private homosexuality enters the brutal arena of public opinion.]

Suddenly Last Summer weaves an interesting set of variations on the theme of exposure for the homosexual artist. Sebastian Venable has always been a private artist, wishing to be "unknown outside of a small coterie." The privacy of Sebastian's art is a corollary to his sense that his art is his expression of his religious vision; for the rest of his experience, living was enough: "his life was his occupation." Yet that life was to be even more private than his work: "He *dreaded, abhorred!*—false values that come from being publicly known, from fame, from personal—exploitation." But Sebastian's private life became a public matter when his cousin/wife witnessed his death and devouring at the hands of adolescent boys Sebastian had sexually exploited. To protect Sebastian's privacy, his mother will have Sebastian's widow lobotomized.

Homosexuality in *Suddenly Last Summer* is linked with Sebastian's brutal, carnivorous sense of life, but it is also linked with Williams's private sexual proclivities. Sebastian connects sex with appetite:

> Cousin Sebastian said he was famished for blonds, he was fed up with the dark ones and was famished for blonds.... [T]hat's how he talked about people, as if they were—items on a menu—.

Donald Spoto argues convincingly for a strong autobiographical element in *Suddenly Last Summer*, nowhere clearer than in this speech. While in Italy in 1948, Williams wrote Donald Windham: "[Prokosch] says that Florence is full of blue-eyed blonds that are very tender hearted and 'not at all mercenary'. We were both getting an appetite for blonds as the Roman gentry are all sort of dusky types." Sebastian's unfeeling sexual exploitation is as much a dramatization of the playwright as is Sebastian's pill-popping and confused sense of private and public personae.

Cat on a Hot Tin Roof, written around the same time as "Hard Candy," is the most vivid dramatic embodiment of Williams's mixed signals regarding homosexuality and his obsession with public exposure. *Cat* takes place in the bedroom once occupied by Jack Straw and Peter Ochello, a room dominated by the large double bed the lovers shared for thirty years. The plantation the ailing Big Daddy now controls, and which is now being fought over by his potential heirs, was inherited from Straw and Ochello. In ways both financial and sexual, the legacy of these two lovers lies at the heart of the play, and the love of Jack Straw and Peter Ochello stands as a counter to the compromised heterosexual relationships we see played out. Their relationship, the reader is told in the stage directions, "*must have involved a tenderness which was uncommon,*" yet the audience never hears the relationship spoken of in positive terms. Straw and Ochello do not carry the freight of negative stereotypes other Williams homosexuals carry: they are not frail like Blanche DuBois's suicidal husband; nor voracious pederasts like Sebastian Venable, the poet-martyr of *Suddenly Last Summer*; nor are they self-hating like Skipper, the other homosexual ghost in *Cat*. Yet, beyond the stage directions, there is no positive language for Straw and Ochello, who become in the action of the play the targets for Brick's homophobic diatribes.

Straw and Ochello's heir was Big Daddy Pollitt, the cigar-smoking, virile patriarch who admits to loving only two things, his "twenty-eight thousand acres of the richest land this side of the Valley Nile!" and his handsome, ex-athlete son, Brick, who has turned into a drunken recluse since the death of his best friend, Skipper, The central scene in the play is a violent confrontation between patriarch and troubled son in which Big Daddy tries to get at the truth of Brick's relationship with Skipper.

Williams's stage direction tells the reader that Big Daddy "*leaves a lot unspoken*" as he tells Brick of his young years as a hobo and of being taken in and given a job by Jack Straw and Peter Ochello. The implication of the stage direction, and other hints Big Daddy gives in the scene, is that homosexual behavior is not alien to Big Daddy, who "knocked around in [his] time." Yet Brick is so terrified of being called "queer" that he cannot listen to what his father is trying to tell him:

> BIG DADDY: . . . I bummed, I bummed this country till I was—
> BRICK: Whose suggestion, who else's suggestion is it?
> BIG DADDY: Slept in hobo jungles and railroad Y's and flophouses in all cities before I—
> BRICK: Oh, *you* think so, too, you call me your son and a queer. Oh! Maybe that's why you put Maggie and me in this room that was Jack Straw's and Peter Ochello's, in which that pair of old sisters slept in a double bed where both of 'em died!
> BIG DADDY: *Now just don't go throwing rocks at—*

The exchange is a brilliant reversal of expectation: the object of suspicion will not listen to expressions of understanding and tolerance, countering them with homophobic ranting. Brick is obsessed, terrified of being called a "queer," and conscious of the irony of being expected to perform sexually in Straw and Ochello's bed. Big Daddy will allow no attacks on Straw and Ochello, but his defense is interrupted by the appearance of Reverend Tooker,

"the living embodiment of the pious, conventional lie," an interruption that suggests that it is the pious conventional lie that for-
bids defense of Straw and Ochello. The interruption is Williams's
choice: it allows Brick's homophobic discourse to dominate the
scene. In addition to "queer[s]" and "old sisters," Brick speaks of
"sodomy," "dirty things," dirty old men," "ducking [*sic*] sissies,"
"unnatural thing," and *"fairies."* Brick's acceptance of the pious
conventional lie is heard in statements which sound like a caricature of the voice of pious respectability: "Big Daddy, you shock
me, Big Daddy, you, you—*shock* me! Talkin' so—casually!—about
a—thing like that." Yet his stated reason for his shock is not moral,
religious, or psychological; it is public opinion: "Don't you know
how people *feel* about things like that? How, how *disgusted* they
are by things like that?" Homosexuality to Brick is terrifying
because it is inevitably public.

> —John M. Clum, "'Something Cloudy, Something Clear': Homo-
> phobic Discourse in Tennessee Williams," *South Atlantic Quarterly*
> 88 (1989): 149–167. Reprinted in *Homosexual Themes in Literary
> Studies,* ed. Wayne R. Dynes and Stephen Donaldson (New York:
> Garland, 1992): 157–159.

STEVEN BRUHM ON HOMOSEXUAL IMAGERY AND ON THE
IMPOSSIBILITY OF HOMOGRAPHESIS

[Steven Bruhm teaches at Mount Saint Vincent University.
He is the author of *Gothic Bodies: The Politics of Pain in
Romantic Fiction.* In this excerpt Bruhm analyzes the significance of Sebastian's *Poems of Summer* as the "queer
meaning" of the play. In the second selection, Bruhm
suggests that Sebastian's homosexual narcissism may be
the very thing that keeps him alive.]

What exactly did Sebastian Venable write in his *Poem of Summer*?
What comprised the body and soul of this brainchild that took nine
months—"the length of a pregnancy"—to produce? We don't
know, of course. Tennessee Williams's *Suddenly Last Summer* simply
tells us that Sebastian, the gay poet murdered before the play

opens, has written a poem each summer for 25 years. We have a
title, but we have no text, a signifier with an ostentatiously absent
signified. Which is interesting, of course, because we also have a
play about a gay man but with no gay man in it: he is absent,
apparitional (to borrow Terry Castle's adjective); he is always
already consumed at the moment we would have him rendered
present so that we may consume him. Like a Foucauldian case
study of the discursive construction of sexuality, Sebastian exists
only as a composite of various testimonies that attempt to define
the poet and, indirectly, the "homosexual." But such an absence
can be productive, and not only for what it tells us about straight
definitions of the gay man. I want to suggest here that while we
can never know the content of Sebastian's *Poems of Summer*, it is
precisely the presence of the poem which can never be read that
marks the queer meaning of *Suddenly Last Summer*, and whose
slippage goes to the heart of Williams's self-representation in the
late 1950s.

Sebastian's silenced poem is crucial to the play not only because
it frames the problem of presence and absence that is central to
the play's representation of the gay man, but also because it raises
the question of homosexual writing, a question that, for Lee
Edelman, is crucial for the 1950s' construction—and destruction—
of gay males. In *Homographesis*, Edelman argues that straight
America during the Cold War was plagued by the feeling that
homosexuals had, on the one hand, infiltrated culture and politics on every level but were, on the other hand, impossible to
detect. Like communists, their very invisibility led them to be
"seen" everywhere. This troubling (in)visibility, he argues, gives rise
to "homographesis," the attempt to posit

> homosexuality as a *legible* phenomenon while simultaneously
> acknowledging the frequency with which it manages to escape
> detection; it constructs male homosexuality in terms of what the
> "public eye" can recognize even as it situates it in an ontolog-
> ical shuttle between perceptual sameness and difference.
> (emphasis added)

In Edelman's analysis, what "the 'public eye' can recognize" is effeminacy, which becomes the diagnostic homographic designation, the
"essential" characteristic of the gay man. The very "difference" of
homosexual maleness can be cognized only by seeing it as similar
to (straight) femininity. And this diagnosis is made possible,

Edelman argues, by a strategy of metaphor: whereas, prior to the late nineteenth century, the sodomite was viewed as an agent whose activities could metonymically be seen to operate anywhere and everywhere, the twentieth-century psychopathologizing of the homosexual reinterpreted "the subject's relation to sexuality . . . as essential or metaphoric." Effeminacy becomes the "visible emblem or metaphor for the 'singular nature' that now defines or identifies a specifically homosexual type of person." Homographesis, the writing of the homosexual into visibility (and consequently into a specific kind of persecution), proceeds by the deployment of metaphors that claim to capture him, embody him, "carry" him "over" in the literal sense of the rhetorical term.

While the competing testimonies of *Suddenly Last Summer* do not portray Sebastian as particularly effeminate, they do draw on legible images of homosexuality that are equally homographic in Edelman's terms: sensitivity, creativity, "*grandeur*," secrecy—in short, all the characteristics of "narcissism." And while Williams never alludes directly to the Narcissus myth in any of its variations, he does use Sebastian for some very telling narcissistic reflections: the gay man in this play is intensely private and antisocial, working in a cloistered atelier so that "no one but he could see" the fruits of his labors; he was "unknown outside a small coterie of friends" and "had not public name as a poet;" more important, he was strongly cathected on his mother—the telltale sign of the homosexual narcissist since Freud—and seemed unable to produce any poetry without her during the summer of his death: "something had broken," Catharine says, "that string of pearls that old mothers hold their sons by like a—sort of a—sort of—*umbilical* cord;" this mother-fixation is stereotypically enhanced by the absence of the father, which mouths the assumption of psychoanalysis in the late 1950s/early 1960s that "a constructive, supportive, warmly related father *precludes* the possibility of a homosexual son;" and finally, Sebastian rejected the Echo-like advances of Catharine as she "made the mistake of responding too much to his kindness, of taking hold of his hand before he'd take hold of [hers], . . . of appreciating his kindness more than he wanted [her] to." Without saying so, Williams draws a textbook study of the kind of homosexual man the Freudian enterprise had identified some forty-five years earlier, the type whose delusions of grandeur result from an inability to cast the mother in the role of sexual otherness, and who instead identifies with her too fully. In the desire to please her, he identifies with her desire, the desire for the male body, for the phallus of another man.

⁓

Williams depicts Sebastian not only as the eater but as the eaten, a victim not only of his own desires but the desires of others: Violet who wants him "chaste," Catharine who wants his sexual friendship, George who wants his inheritance, Cukrowicz who wants his trust fund. Indeed, it is *Suddenly Last Summer's* major social criticism that Sebastian's fatal behavior is not metaphor but synecdoche, a signifier of *everyone's* opportunism. As Catharine tells that other great predator, the lobotomist Cukrowicz, "we all use each other and that's what we think of as love, and not being able to use each other is what's—*hate*." If the destruction of the turtles metaphorizes Sebastian's treatment of other human beings it also employs the homosexual to figure synecdochically the non-homosexual, the social, the Garden District of New Orleans. Egomaniacal grandeur is morally no less reprehensible here than it is in Sebastian, but it is divested of its supposedly homosexual psychic configurations. Rather, the play has as its subject matter the impossibility of a homographesis that will write the homosexual in a complete, omniscient, essentializing narrative.

This inability, this gap in the central metaphor of the play, creates in Sebastian an effect akin to narcissism. As Julia Kristeva, following Lacan, has emphasized, the narcissism of the mirror stage centers on a fundamental emptiness in which the self is located where it is not. Narcissism emphasizes the *difference* in a subjectivity thought to be characterized by a self-enclosed sameness. For Ovid's Narcissus, this difference is profoundly productive of homoeros: Narcissus falls in love with another man, a man he cognizes only as other; moreover, as Tireseas tells us, Narcissus will live as long as he does not know that the image in the water is himself. In other words, homoerotic desire does not paralyze him but rather engages him, for the first time, in the love of another, and the maintenance of the erotic life depends here on the maintenance of homosexual desire, the cessation of which means death. This self-love, which is simultaneously the erotic cathexis on another, becomes in later treatments (the most famous being those of Plotinus and the Schlegels) *the* metaphor for philosophical and poetic textual creativity. It is only with the interruption of narcissistic desire—that is, desire for the other man—that Narcissus stops cathecting, stops creating, stops living. And the same is true for Sebastian Venable. Catharine tells us that he was "Completing—a sort of!—*image!*—he had of himself as a sort of!—*sacrifice* to a!—*terrible* sort of a— . . . God," the God of the Encantadas, the God whose image he had sought. But while the egomaniacal completion of the image results in his death—that is, Narcissus drowns—the play asks us to consider Sebastian before the completion, when his image of himself was still presumably fragmentary, differentiated, split. In this Sebastian we see the productive poet; in this Sebastian we see the active homosexual; and, most interestingly, in this Sebastian we see the man capable of acts of kindness to others, as he rescues Catharine from her disastrous scene at the Mardi Gras Ball. Thus, in Williams's intervention in the homographic metaphors of psychoanalysis, homosexual desire is not egomaniacal and self-destructive so much as the *end* of desire is deadly; in fact, the desire for his own divine image and for the sameness of another male body is directly connected to the awareness of and concern for the other. In *Suddenly Last Summer*, it is the end of homosexual narcissism, of blond ambition, that heralds death.

—Steven Bruhm, "Blond Ambition: Tennessee Williams's Homographesis," *Essays in Theatre/Etudes Theatrales* 14, no. 2 (May 1996): 97–100.

Jacqueline O'Connor on a Question of Sanity and on Truth as Illusion

[Jacqueline O'Connor is assistant professor of English at Stephen F. Austin State University where she teaches drama, American literature, and composition. She has published articles on David Rabe, Anna Cora Mowatt, and Tennessee Williams. In this reading O'Connor discusses how, because we cannot know if Catharine's story is true or untrue, we cannot know whether she is sane or insane. In the second extract O'Connor analyzes the characters and which version of the story they choose to believe about Sebastian's death.]

Suddenly Last Summer takes place in the jungle-like garden of the Venable home. The setting recalls the quotation from the Song of Solomon that Williams uses for the epigraph to *The Two-Character Play:* "A garden enclosed is my sister . . . a spring shut up, a fountain sealed." The film version of *Suddenly* (screenplay by Gore Vidal) moves some of the action to the private asylum where Catharine Holly has been confined; contrasting the two versions highlights the stage version's success in conveying an atmosphere of confinement, for the film seems more mobile, although it contains scenes in the institution, the ultimate location of confinement.

Williams also uses aspects of the total institution to convey Catharine's predicament, the most obvious being the references to various forms of treatment: drug therapy, insulin shock treatments, electric shock treatments, and lobotomy. When Catharine appears at the opening of scene two, with the nun who accompanies her from St. Mary's, her first action onstage has her taking a cigarette from a box on the table and lighting it. Goffman lists smoking as one of the "minor activities that one can execute on one's own on the outside," which becomes, in the institution, an act requiring permission from the staff. ⟨. . .⟩ The sister repeatedly demands that Catharine put out the cigarette, ignoring pleas from Catharine that their removal from hospital grounds might allow for a relaxation of hospital policy. Catharine makes no headway with the line of argument, however, and shows her frustration by extinguishing the cigarette in the nun's outstretched hand. This establishes Catharine's character as willful, while highlighting the personal restrictions of asylum life. Even when away from the hospital, the patient's most ordinary privileges are limited by the restrictions of the total institution. Catharine's behavior is more understandable in light of the claim that Goffman makes: "Many of these potential gratifications are carved out of the flow of support that the inmate had previously taken for granted." Such common acts as smoking a cigarette take on heightened significance, "re-establishing relationships with the whole lost world and assuaging withdrawal symptoms from it and one's lost self." Thus,

Catharine's first act in the play signals her desire to take control of her environment and assert herself as an autonomous member of society. The nun's refusal to allow this freedom, and the doctor's subsequent granting permission to smoke, signifies their different perspectives on Catharine's role.

~

The determination to choose one story over another, as well as the defensiveness of the one deemed mad because of the content of the account, is a source of tension in ⟨. . .⟩ *Suddenly Last Summer*, once again the sanity and the confinement of the presumed mad person depends on the story that is central to the play. An early draft, in which Catharine is named Valerie, focuses on her propensity to chatter, for she tells the sister who accompanies her from the institution: "I can't stop talking, I never could when I'm nervous." Immediately after this, she informs the doctor that her nails have been cut to keep her from hurting herself during the convulsions that occur after shock treatment. The doctor then asks the sister, "Isn't she off shock now?" and Valerie replies: "You can ask me, I can answer. I'm off it now." This version emphasizes that the girl is ready and anxious to talk about her treatment, and to tell the story that has been her undoing; indeed, she will persist in telling her version of the truth no matter what: "They can't cut the true story out of my brain." Also: "I'm going to get the truth serum again I know. But it doesn't change the story." A longer speech about the story she is prepared to tell reveals her inner wrestling with the narrative of her cousin's fate:

> I can't falsify it. . . . It's no pleasure having to repeat the same story over and over, but even if I wished not to, even if I wished to falsify it, what could I say? . . . I just can't help repeating what actually did happen, it just—spills out!—each time!—the truth about what happened.

Although Williams deletes these comments from the final version, he retains the concentration on truth; the word "truth" is repeated fifteen times, mostly by Catharine, and it is echoed by the doctor in the final line of the play: "I think we ought at least to consider the possibility that the girl's story could be true." Truth has "the last word." Its constant recurrence emphasizes its significance. Defining the truth may well determine Catharine's future.

In the earlier version, Valerie [Catharine] sums up the major conflict of the play when she tells the doctor, "I'm not mad. It's just that I witnessed something no one will believe and they'd rather think I'm mad than to believe it." Her statement illustrates one of the most common determinations of madness in Williams's plays: whether an implausible story is accepted by the other characters. The predicament she describes could be that of either Blanche (although Blanche is more than a witness to the violent act in *Streetcar*), or Valerie [Catharine], for the latter assesses the truth as unbelievable; the only option for those who deny this truth is to proclaim the teller mad. In both plays, the madwoman insists on telling a story whose premise is unacceptable, thus resulting in that woman's expulsion from society. Allan Ingram in *The Madhouse of Language* writes: "one prime feature of the madman's discourse is obsession, the returning always to one subject of conversation." Catharine's obsession with the story of Sebastian's death causes her to return to that subject incessantly; as Violet tells the Doctor, Catharine "babbles" it at every opportunity. Although we wonder about her sanity, we cannot deny her obsessive discourse.

In a review of the original production of *Suddenly*, Richard Watts describes the action as "in large part a drama of two speeches, the first by the mother of a dead poet, who is certain that a young woman has caused his death, and the other by the possibly insane girl, who gives her own version of what happened." Like the rape in *Streetcar*, Sebastian's death is also a story of violence, as well as a narrative that maligns the character of the central male figure of the play. In *Suddenly*, however, Sebastian is dead, and cannot refute the tale's truth, as Stanley does. At *Suddenly*'s opening, Catharine is already confined for telling the story, and so the action contrasts with that of *Streetcar*: it moves toward the possible release of Catharine at the end of the play. The account that Catharine gives of Sebastian's death unequivocally provides the only reason for Catharine's confinement, although she does exhibit peculiar behavior: she causes a scene at a Mardi Gras ball, and she shows unusual distance from her own feelings by using the third-person in her diary. But her horrifying tale, with the aspersions it casts on Sebastian's character, sends her to the asylum and results in her receiving various treatments for memory suppression, attempts designed to prevent her from repeating her version of his murder.

The story prompts Violet Venable to seek the assistance of Doctor Cukrowicz, who performs lobotomies. If he can determine that Catharine has fabricated the story, he will perform the operation. In this play, two men represent the deciding consensus of the community: the doctor, and Catharine's brother, George. Unlike *Streetcar*, in *Suddenly* we do not know if the story is true, but we do get to hear Catharine tell it, and we also witness the reaction of her audience. In *Suddenly*, the story has strikingly different effects on the characters who hear it: Catharine's narrative sends Violet into a rage, demanding that the story be excised from her niece's brain; however, it seems to convince the doctor, who is at least ready to accept the possibility of its truth. George seems more convinced, even though his position throughout the play has been on the side of his aunt, since he wants the money from the inheritance.

These two plays make clear, in different ways, that the characters' ability to convince others of the truth of certain situations does not depend on whether these events actually occurred. Ultimately, this is because the line between truth and fiction often blurs. Tom Wingfield's description of the play he narrates gives a hint of this, when he claims it to be "truth in the pleasant guise of illusion," and Blanche provides another twist when she speaks of telling "what ought to be truth." Both *Streetcar* and *Suddenly* raise the possibility of confinement for a major character; what becomes clear, however, is that the confinement is decided in part because these women have forced others to consider how the truth might be determined.

One important distinction is noteworthy in a comparison of the storytelling aspects of the plays. We might contrast their dramatic progression by saying that Blanche moves toward madness, and Catharine moves away from it toward her possible release. Blanche's last long speech is not about the past, as the others have been, but about the future, a virtual prediction of her own death. In contrast, Catharine's longest speech occurs at the end of the play; she does not appear in the first scene, and in that scene Mrs. Venable controls the doctor's perceptions of Sebastian's character and life. Violet makes a reference to "talking the ears off a donkey," indicating an awareness of her verbosity. When the group has gathered to hear Catherine's version of the events in Cabeza de Lobo, Violet repeatedly interrupts Catharine's speeches, attempting to adjust or deny the girl's declarations. Finally the doctor halts the interruptions, and demands that Catharine be allowed to continue her narrative without interruption. Not only is the monologue the dramatic climax of the play, it allows the revelation of the story that has caused Catharine's confinement, a narrative that Violet seeks to silence. The release of this story to the ears of the family and the doctor (and the audience) thwarts Violet's effort to suppress it, and may lead to Catharine's release.

—Jacqueline O'Connor, *Dramatizing Dementia: Madness in the Plays of Tennessee Williams* (Bowling Green, Ohio: Bowling Green State University Popular Press, 1997): 23–24, 64–66.

Plot Summary of
The Glass Menagerie

The Glass Menagerie earned Williams the epithet "dramatist of frustration." The play is a tale of three people trapped in a world of their own illusions. Tom Winfield, the narrator through whose memories the characters and plot are revealed, is a poet and a dreamer and, in a rudimentary sense, Tennessee Williams himself. Winfield tries to escape the harsh reality of tenement life by immersing himself in D. H. Lawrence novels and the movies. In **scene one** Tom begins his story from the fire escape outside the Wingfield apartment window; the 1940s and World War II have begun: The memories Tom shares describe the Depression years of the 1930s. His "poet's weakness for symbols" will shape the truth of his memories through illusions. His mother, Amanda, enthralled by her fantasies of her youth as a southern belle, tells them the oft-repeated story of the 17 "gentleman callers" she entertained one Sunday afternoon on Blue Mountain. Amanda thinks her daughter's life will be transformed if she will complete a typing course (**scene two**), but Laura is uninterested, preferring instead to polish her collection of glass animal figurines, her glass menagerie. The pressure of the typing course made her sick and she now only pretends to attend, wandering in the park each day until it's time to come home. But Amanda is rightly concerned about Laura's future: Without a career, marriage is the only choice.

In **scene three** Tom, as narrator, is amused by Amanda's new obsession to find Laura a husband. He reenters the play to argue furiously with his mother, stopping only when Laura intercedes. He gets up abruptly to leave the apartment and his coat knocks the shelf holding Laura's menagerie to the floor, shattering the collection. It seems as if this might mark a turning point of some kind in Laura's life, but Laura seems to have little capacity to react, much less change. Tom returns, drunk (**scene four**), and Laura tries without success to get Tom to apologize to their mother. One may wonder why he came back at all. Tom eventually apologizes and Amanda responds, "My devotion has made me a witch and so I make myself hateful to my children." There is no response possible to this. Tom explains that his nightly movie-going satisfies some need for adventure, but Amanda reminds him that other men find adventure in their work. Amanda makes a bargain: She will not interfere with Tom's activities if he will provide a man for Laura.

Winter has turned to spring as **scene five** begins, and Amanda is still nagging Tom, now to become a CPA. Tom steps onto the fire escape to narrate for us the coming of World War II; Amanda joins him and he tells her that he has at last invited a young man, Jim O'Connor, to dinner the next evening. His mother is ecstatic, but Tom admits that he has not told Jim about Laura, about her peculiar immersion "in a world of her own, a world of little glass ornaments." Tom observes that Jim was a symbolic figure, "the long-delayed but always expected something that we live for." In **scene six** he describes the reality: Jim is a high school hero who, six years after graduation, has a modest position at the Continental Shoemakers warehouse and no prospects for anything more substantial. Laura prepares for his arrival; stage directions tell us that a "fragile, unearthly prettiness has come out in Laura: she is like a piece of translucent glass touched by light, given a momentary radiance, not actual, not lasting." Amanda, too, prepares for the arrival of this gentleman caller, determined to snare him either with Laura's loveliness or by the force of her own formidable charm. Amanda reveals to Laura, just before he arrives, Jim's identity. Laura becomes physically ill with fright. When he arrives Jim hardly notices Amanda; he is more interested in talking with Tom. Tom reveals that, instead of paying the light bill, he has joined the Union of Merchant Seamen. Laura cowers in the kitchen while Amanda entertains Jim with nonstop chatter, which seems to charm him as much as it embarrasses Tom. Eventually, Tom helps Laura into the living room where she remains, huddled on the couch, throughout dinner (**scene seven**).

Dinner begins and the lights go out. Referring to the war, Tom remarks that "nowadays the world is lit by lightning," but here the reality of an unpaid bill is less poetic. Amanda gives Jim a candelabrum she has saved from the burned Church of the Heavenly Rest and tells him to keep Laura company in the living room. Her plan or trap may yet succeed. Jim is charming and seems to want Laura's admiration as much as Amanda had wanted his. Laura brings out their high school yearbook (*The Torch*) and Jim treats this record of his past glory with a certain reverence. But Jim is not as detached from the present as Laura. He has plans, albeit naive ones, for the future, which he shares with Laura. He is kind to Laura and pays attention to her glass collection, even to her fantasy about the unicorn, which "loves light." He asks Laura to dance. While dancing they bump the table that holds the collection and the unicorn falls to the floor and the horn breaks off, making it like all the other horses. The symbolism may seem heavy-handed but the affect is poignant and powerful. Jim blames himself, but Laura seems unperturbed. He kisses her and instantly realizes that he has overstepped some boundary. He tells her that he will not return to see her, that he is engaged to another girl. Williams writes, "The holy candles on the altar of Laura's face have been snuffed out." She is speechless with shock. But the evening seems, ultimately, more of a failure to Amanda than to Laura. Amanda turns her rage upon Tom, accusing him of deliberately deceiving them both. Tom, intending only to escape to the movies, leaves the apartment and never returns. Amanda calls after him, "Go to the moon you selfish dreamer!" But they have all embraced dreams and illusions.

As the play closes Tom talks about his travels since leaving St. Louis, admitting that "cities swept about [him] like dead leaves . . . torn from the branches." Tom's desire for escape and adventure seems equal to his capacity for self-pity. He has been unable to break his emotional ties with his family, particularly his attachment to his sister. At the last moment Laura blows out the candles and the stage is dark, perhaps indicating that Tom is at last rid of the guilty burden of his memory of Laura. ❀

List of Characters in
The Glass Menagerie

Amanda Wingfield is Laura's mother. Her husband long ago deserted the family, but she displays a photo of him as a reminder to all of his good looks and charm. She holds delusions of her past as a southern belle as well as delusions about Laura's future as a secretary and the prospect of numerous "gentleman callers." She also has unrealistic expectations for her son, Tom, who, she thinks, could achieve a better position at the warehouse where he works. In many ways Amanda is like Laura. She lives in a world of her own construction that has little to do with the reality of all their circumstances. She persuades Tom to invite a friend from the warehouse home for dinner and then imagines that a romantic relationship is developing between Laura and the young man. When she finds out that the man is engaged she is furious with Tom. But Amanda is also an admirable character, tender toward Laura and never giving up hope for the best for her family.

Laura Wingfield is Amanda's daughter and Tom's younger sister. She is crippled by a childhood illness and wears a leg brace. Extremely self-conscious, she is housebound and collects glass animal figurines. Her favorite is a unicorn, a creature we recognize as a symbol of her isolation within the dream life she sustains and her "freakish" difference from other people. Jim seems to recognize this in the nickname he gives her, "Blue Roses." She is fragile and childlike, withdrawn into an internal world she has constructed for herself. She is neither strong, like her mother, nor able to escape, like Tom.

Tom Wingfield is Amanda's son and Laura's older brother. A warehouse worker, he is much like his runaway father, whom he describes as "a telephone man who fell in love with long distance." He writes poetry and dreams of getting away from the family, talking frequently about rejoining the merchant marines. He loves his sister and is the sole support of the family. Tom is the narrator of the play; his tone is sentimental and what we know about the family is only what he chooses to tell us. Tom's story is both personal and symbolic of the greater social ethos at a time in history just before World War II, which would consume the futures of all young men such as Tom.

Jim O'Connor is the rather ordinary young man that Tom brings to dinner one evening. Tom introduces him to us as an emissary from reality. But the play is built on illusion, and Jim, although he works hard in order to succeed, is likely to accomplish very little in life. Laura remembers Jim from high school and he seems to her as charming now as she found him then. Jim is flattered and pleased with himself. He dances with Laura and kisses her, then dismisses her with the news that he is already engaged to another girl. Amanda had hoped that his attentions were a sign of romance for Laura and is, perhaps rightly, furious with Tom for bringing an engaged man to dinner. ✿

Critical Views of
The Glass Menagerie

JOHN GASSNER ON A SYNTHESIS OF SYMPATHY AND
OBJECTIVITY

[John Gassner (1903–1967) published widely on American
theater. His works include *Theatre at the Crossroads: Plays and
Playwrights of the Mid-Century American Stage* and *Dramatic Soundings.* In this excerpt Gassner discusses Williams's
transformation of base reality into theatrical poesy.]

The plays that thrust Tennessee Williams into the limelight have much
in common besides their clear focus and economical construction.
Both *The Glass Menagerie* and *A Streetcar Named Desire* transmute the
base metal of reality into theatrical and, not infrequently, verbal
poetry, and both supplement the action with symbolic elements of
mood and music. A major theme is southern womanhood helpless in
the grip of the presently constituted world, while its old world of social
position and financial security is a Paradise Lost. But differences of
emphasis and style make the two dramas distinct.

The Glass Menagerie is a memory play evoked in the comments
of a narrator, the poet Tom, who is now in the merchant marine,
and in crucial episodes from his family life. The form departs from
the "fourth wall" convention of realistic dramaturgy and suggests
Japanese Noh-drama, in which story consists mostly of remembered
fragments of experience. If Williams had had his way with the
Broadway production, *The Glass Menagerie* would have struck its
public as even more unconventional, since his text calls for the use
of a screen on which pictures and legends are to be projected. Dis-
regarded by the producer-director Eddie Dowling, these stage directions nevertheless appear in the published play. They strike the
writer of this article as redundant and rather precious; the young
playwright was straining for effect without realizing that his simple
tale, so hauntingly self-sufficient, needs no adornment.

As plainly stated by Tom, the background is a crisis in society,
for the depression decade is teetering on the brink of the second
World War. His tale belongs to a time "when the huge middle-class
of America was matriculating in a school for the blind," when "their

eyes had failed them, or they had failed their eyes, and so they were having their fingers pressed forcibly down on the fiery Braille alphabet of a dissolving economy," while in Spain there was Guernica. But his memory invokes his home life and the provocations that finally sent him to sea. In episodes softened by the patina of time and distance he recalls the painful shyness of his lovable crippled sister, Laura, and the tragicomic efforts of his mother, Amanda, to marry her off, as well as his own desperation as an underpaid shoe-company clerk. The climax comes when, nagged by the desperate mother, Tom brings Laura a "gentleman caller" who turns out to be engaged to another girl.

Without much more story than this, Williams achieved a remarkable synthesis of sympathy and objectivity by making three-dimensional characters out of Tom's family and the gangling beau, who is trying to pull himself out of the rut of a routine position and recover his self-esteem as a schoolboy success. The carping mother could have easily become a caricature, especially when she remembers herself as a southern belle instead of a woman deserted by her husband, a telephone man who "fell in love with long distance" but who probably found an incitement in his wife's pretensions. She is redeemed for humanity by her solicitude for her children, her laughable but touching effort to sell a magazine subscription over the telephone at dawn, and her admission that the unworldly Laura must get a husband if she is to escape the fate of the "little birdlike women without any nest" Amanda has known in the South. And Laura, too shy even to take a course in typewriting after the first lesson, acquits herself with sweet dignity and becoming stoicism when let down by her first and only gentleman caller; she is an unforgettable bit of Marie Laurence in painting. At the same time, however, Williams knows that pity for the halt and blind must not exclude a sense of reality, that Tom's going out into the world was a necessary and wholesome measure of self-preservation; it is one of humanity's inalienable traits and obligations to try to save itself as best it can. Although Tom will never forget Laura and the candles she blew out, he is now part of the larger world that must find a common salvation in action, "for nowadays the world is lit by lightning."

—John Gassner, "Tennessee Williams: Dramatist of Frustration," College English 10, no. 10 (October 1948): 1–7.

WALTER KERR ON THE FAILURE OF CONCLUSIONS

[Walter Kerr (1913–1966) was a prominent American theater critic and author. His works include *The Decline of Pleasure, How Not to Write a Play,* and *The Theater in Spite of Itself.* In this excerpt Kerr complains that the endings of the plays suggest Williams's failure of dramaturgical courage.]

The failures of Tennessee Williams are worth talking about. Mr. Williams, it seems to me, is the finest playwright now working in the American theater; every failure he has represents a real loss not only to himself but to all the rest of us. When so substantial and exhilarating a talent appears, the hope must be for the largest possible body of durable work.

Almost alone among his contemporaries, and without wholly shaking off the realistic tradition that is ours, Williams sees and writes as an artist and a poet. He makes plays out of images, catching a turn of life while it is still fluid, still immediate, before it has been sterilized by reflection. Arthur Miller may sometimes build a better play, but he builds it out of bricks; Williams is all flesh and blood. He writes with his eyes and his ears where other men are content to pick their brains—poetry with them is an overlay of thought, not a direct experience—and his best plays emerge in the theater full-bodied, undissected, so kinetic you can touch them.

The curious thing about Williams' lapses is that they seem to represent a conscious straining away from the virtues that are most naturally his, a rebellion against self that takes the form of wanting to shatter—or escape from—the mirror he has taken such pains to perfect. Life is his for the patient echoing; he occasionally seems to want, wantonly, to silence the echo.

The least of his vices, but one that has been with him from the beginning, is his inability—or refusal—to conclude anything, to find endings for his narratives that will embrace, take account of, and face up to the materials out of which he has begun them. *The Glass Menagerie* simply stops; the play has been so accurate and so touching that we do not really mind. *A Streetcar Named Desire* escapes into the heroine's insanity; the play remains thrilling, but this is to wash out the struggle rather than resolve it.

—Walter Kerr, "Playwrights," *Pieces at Eight* (1957): 125–134. Reprinted in *The Chelsea House Library of Literary Criticism: Twentieth-Century American Literature,* vol. 7, ed. Harold Bloom (New York: Chelsea House Publishers, 1988): 4311–4312.

Arthur Ganz on the Influence of D. H. Lawrence

[Arthur Ganz is the author of *Pinter, a Collection of Critical Essays, Realms of the Self: Variations on a Theme in Modern Drama,* and a critical volume on the works of George Bernard Shaw. Here Ganz views Williams's use Lawrence's theme of the awakening of life in *The Glass Menagerie.*]

To understand this violence in Williams' work we must first look at his gentlest plays, those in which the virtuous are rewarded, for here is most directly revealed the morality by which the guilty are later so terribly condemned. Surprisingly, one of Williams' most significant plays is an indifferent and undramatic one-acter about the death of D. H. Lawrence, only slightly redeemed by the audacious and successful title, *I Rise in Flame, Cried the Phoenix.* The play is significant because it gives us the central fact we must have to understand Williams' work, the nature of his literary parentage. In art, a son must seek out a father who will give him what he needs. Williams needed a rationale for the sexual obsessions that dominate his work, and it was this that Lawrence seemed to give him. In the Preface to *I Rise in Flame* Williams wrote, "Lawrence felt the mystery and power of sex, as the primal life urge, and was the lifelong adversary of those who wanted to keep the subject locked away in the cellars of prudery," and in the play he makes Frieda exclaim, "You just don't know. The meaning of Lawrence escapes you. In all of his work he celebrates the body."

Whether or not Williams assesses Lawrence correctly is, for an understanding of Williams' own work, irrelevant. The important thing is that from a very early point in his career (*I Rise in Flame* dates from 1941) Williams saw Lawrence as the great writer who "celebrates the body" and apparently saw himself as that writer's disciple. Like many disciples, however, Williams introduced his own variations on the master's doctrine. Williams betrayed Lawrence primarily by extending the approval of Lawrentian doctrine to areas of sexual experience beyond the normal, but first he did so by basing a very bad play on one of Lawrence's short stories.

The play, called *You Touched Me* from Lawrence's story of that title, is an early work, copyrighted in 1942. Although it shows little of the doctrinal variation on which Williams' later work is based, the distortions that were introduced as the story was transformed into a play are highly revealing. In addition, *You Touched Me* is important for establishing the structural pattern of two of Williams' most attractive plays, *The Glass Menagerie* and *The Rose Tattoo*. ⟨. . .⟩

Although Williams has distorted Lawrence's work by sentimentalizing it and by introducing into it caricatures of frigidity and impotence, he is genuinely sympathetic to its real theme, the awakening of life, and particularly sexual life, in one who had previously been dead to it. In both the play and the story, Hadrian (the conquering emperor from the warm South) defeats the forces of sterility and rouses Matilda to new life. It was this action, which Williams sees as profoundly good, that he developed in this early play and then made the center of two of his most pleasing works. ⟨. . .⟩

The figure of Laura in *The Glass Menagerie* has clearly been developed from that of Matilda of *You Touched Me*, who is described by Williams as having "the delicate, almost transparent quality of glass." Both are shy, fragile creatures, remote from the life around them. But where Hadrian awakens Matilda and brings her back to life, Laura's gentleman caller gives her only a momentary glimpse of normal life before she drifts back into the fantasy world of glass animals. In Williams' moral system the rejection of life is the greatest crime, and those guilty of it are visited by the kind of punishment that falls upon Blanche DuBois in *Streetcar* and Sebastian Venable in *Suddenly Last Summer*. Laura, however, is innocent; she does not reject but rather is rejected, not because of her limp, which does not exist in "Portrait of a Girl in Glass," Williams' own short story upon which he based his play, but because she is the sensitive, misunderstood exile, a recurrent character in Williams' work, one of the fugitive kind, who are too fragile to live in a malignant world.

—Arthur Ganz, "The Desperate Morality of the Plays of Tennessee Williams," *American Scholar* 31 (Spring 1962): 278–294.

Ruby Cohn on Sublimating Animal Drives into Esthetics

[Ruby Cohn is the author of several volumes of criticism on the plays of Samuel Beckett, as well as *Modern Shakespeare Offshoots, Disjecta: Miscellaneous Writings and a Dramatic Fragment,* and *Around the Absurd.* In this excerpt Cohn discusses quality and power of the illusions that shape the lives of the Wingfields.]

As far back as high school, sensitive Laura was attracted to worldly Jim. Neither a gentleman nor a caller on Laura, the "gentleman caller" mouths clichés of practicality and progress, but his actual career has been a constant retrogression from its high school pinnacle. At the warehouse, Jim evidently uses Tom to recall his high school glory, and in the apartment Jim audibly uses Laura to bolster his sagging self-confidence. Reduced to stale jokes, sports reports, and makeshift psychology, Jim boasts: "I'm not made of glass." (as opposed to the story's less pointed: "I'm not made of eggs!"). However, we can read his fragility through his veneer of psychology, electrodynamics, and public speaking. While dancing with Laura, Jim bumps into a table, breaking the horn of Laura's glass unicorn. As even Jim knows, unicorns are "extinct in the modern world." In the remainder of the scene, Jim virtually breaks Laura, a girl in glass, who lives on imagination and is therefore almost extinct in the modern world. After Jim pays attention to Laura with well-worn clichés—"I'm glad to see that you have a sense of humor." "Did anybody ever tell you that you were pretty?" "I'm talking to you sincerely."—after he kisses her, he reveals that he will not call again because he is engaged to Betty. By the time Amanda intrudes upon the intimacy of Laura and Jim, the brief romance is over. Vulnerable as Jim is in the wider world, he has been injurious to the world of the glass menagerie. The Gentleman Caller of the old South has been replaced by a pathetic shipping clerk of industrial St. Louis, and even he has other allegiances.

More complex than either Jim or Laura, Tom evolves considerably from the narrator of the short story. Designated as a poet in the final version of the play, Tom carries Williams' lyric flights, his verbal creation of atmosphere, and his ironic commentary upon the action. Unlike Wilder's State Manager, Tom remains a character in his own right—fond of his sister, ambiguous about his mother, and eager to follow in his father's escapist footsteps. As Laura is symbolized by her glass unicorn, Tom is symbolized by his movies, which we know only through dialogue. He explains movies to his mother as sublimated adventure, but by the time Jim comes to the house, Tom is tired of vicarious adventures: "People go to the *movies* instead of *moving*. . . . I'm tired of the movies and I'm about to move!" Tom's final speech tells us how far he had moved, and yet he has been unable to escape Proustian recollections of his sister, which are inevitably triggered by colored glass or music.

Though Narrator Tom closes *The Glass Menagerie* on our view of Laura blowing out her candles in a world lit by lightning, the stage viability of the play has always rested upon the character of Amanda. No longer the mere martinet of the short story, she possesses as many qualities "to love and pity . . . as to laugh at." She speaks the most distinctive as well as the most extensive dialogue of the play. It is Amanda who names Laura's collection a "glass menagerie," in which animal drives are frozen into esthetic objects, and it is she who longs for gentleman callers in an ungentle world. At once nostalgic about her genteel past and minimally practical about the sordid present, she punctuates her drawling elegance with sharp questions and terse commands. She recalls every detail of the balls of her youth, and she goes into absurd physiological detail about the daily lives, and especially meals, of her children. In the final version of the play, Williams heightens the Southern quality of her speech, increases her use of "honey" to Laura, her nagging of Tom, and her repetitions. The cumulative effect of these final revisions (particularly the added opening lines about her rejection at church) is to endear her to us, and to evoke pity for the garrulous mother, as for the timid daughter.

After the Gentleman Caller leaves, near the end of the play, Amanda accuses Tom: "You live in a dream; you manufacture illusions!" But the play's pathos arises from the illusions manufactured by *all* the characters. Though the glass menagerie is most directly relevant to Laura, all four characters have sublimated their animal drives into esthetics. Laura has her glass animals, Tom his movies and poems, Amanda her jonquil-filled memories distorted into hopes, and Jim his baritone clichés of progress.

The Glass Menagerie has often been called Chekhovian in its atmospheric rendition of a dying aristocracy. As the last scene opens, a blackout pointedly occurs while Jim and Amanda toast the Old South. What dies into darkness, however, is not a class but a frail feminine household, and we do not feel, as in Chekhov's plays, that the household represents a class.

—Ruby Cohn, "The Garrulous Grotesques of Tennessee Williams," *Dialogue in American Drama* (1971): 97–98.

Nancy M. Tischler on Tom as a Man of Imagination

[Nancy M. Tischler is professor of English at Pennsylvania State University. She is the author of critical volumes on the works of Tennessee Williams and Dorothy L. Sayers, as well as *Black Masks: Negro Characters in Modern Southern Fiction*. In this excerpt Tischler explores the way in which Tom, like many of Williams's characters, must separate from the mother-figure.]

All that is wrong with *Battle of Angels* makes increasingly obvious all that is right with *The Glass Menagerie*. In Williams' own terms, he is now being honest instead of artificial, writing from his heart rather than his head, using his own life as his book. Again basing the story on a self-portrait, he is this time less mythic and intellectual and defensive and pretentious. Instead of Valentine Xavier, he is simple Tom Wingfield, hardly an elaborate mask for Tom Williams. The problem basic to the play is again the hesitation to cross a threshold—this time between adolescence and youth, dependence and independence. The trap of love is again sprung by an older woman, but this time she is honestly the mother, not Venus, the Virgin Mary, Proserpine, and Eurydice. Again the young man escapes and must escape from the tender trap in order to live. But this time all of the social world need not lumber after him to destroy him for his apostasy. The punishment lies not in a lynch mob but in the pain of his memories. The love Tom feels for his mother and his sister is much more real and much more demanding than the combination of sex and compassion Val feels for Lady and the other lost females. The simple tale of a supper for a gentleman caller and an anguished leap for freedom needs no mythic under-girding because it is true and natural and universal. Amanda is by her very nature not merely Tom's mother: she is everyone's mother.

The circumstances are much less disguised and idealized than in *Battle of Angels*. The apartment parallels Willliams' sombre mem-ories of St. Louis, the girl polishing her glass animals closely fol-lows his portraits of his sister Rose before her mental breakdown, and the mother is clearly Williams' own mother with her memo-ries of Mississippi and of youth and springtime and happiness. The major change is his removal of his hated father, who is now but a smiling picture symbolic of the love of long distance. But this change is useful in allowing Williams to avoid a portrayal he was not yet prepared to encounter, to simplify the story, and to inten-sify Amanda's demands, her paranoia, and to help explain Tom's guilt. The alteration of Rose's infirmity to a physical one does not changer her role drastically from that she has played in his life; and she still retains some of that withdrawal from reality that was the clue to her increasing schizophrenia.

Thus, in *The Glass Menagerie*, Tennessee Williams used the very antithesis of the method he had employed for *Battle of Angels*. Instead of constructing this play, he revealed and slightly ordered his own memories. In a sense, he found this easier because he was dealing with his past in *The Glass Menagerie*, while in *Battle of Angels* he had striven to justify and idealize his present and his future. Where he strove to make *Menagerie* more significant by relating it to the Depression and the growing violence abroad, his prose sounds ponderous and irrelevant to the play's tone. His sentimentality at the end is effective enough because it grows out of the deliberately ironic tone Tom has been using as a defense in most of the story. But the excessively arty stage directions reveal the same tendency toward overemphasis so glaringly evident in *Battle of Angels*.

It is far easier to understand Tom's need to escape Amanda and her smothering motherhood than it is to see the archetypal poet's need to escape love and society. The terms of *The Glass Menagerie* are more concretely stated and the conclusions more acceptable: a man of imagination seldom finds fulfillment in a shoe factory; a boy seldom becomes a man under the watchful eye of a domi-neering mother; the break with the past is always painful for the sensitive man; and there is health in this drive to preserve one's integrity and develop to one's maturity regardless of the demands of the family.

Williams has used the tension between self-fulfillment and contribution to the family as the core of several of his plays. Apparently he has found that a man who loves his family never really escapes it. Bad plays like *Moony's Kid Don't Cry* and *The Rose Tattoo* are built on this theme, but good ones are as well (*A Streetcar Named Desire* and *Cat on a Hot Tin Roof*). He finds a resolution of sorts in *Night of the Iguana*, where the grandfather and the daughter can make a home in one another's hearts without demanding permanence or needing to escape (as he and his grandfather did). But even as late as *The Seven Descents of Myrtle*, the mother continues to rule the son, here to the extent that he becomes a transvestite in his effort to accept her personality.

This eternal struggle to cut the umbilical cord, underlying almost all of Williams' work, explains a number of his related ideas. The separation from the mother-figure parallels the separation from society and its values. Amanda represents the ideals of the Old South, the Puritan tradition, and a kind of meaningless conformity that destroys the individual without the consequence of enriching the world. In seeing Amanda, we understand the real reason for the angry attacks on conformists, church people, and small-town tyrants. Val is obviously the Romantic ideal that Tom pictures as he makes his escape out of ugliness, censorship, repression, and stifling love into a world of adventure, rootlessness, and moral anarchy. The artist, as he perceives him, lives in a world of polarities: masculine and feminine, past and present, conformity and nonconformity, control and chaos. He also discovers his world is full of paradoxes: love is a weapon women use to unman the male; compassion is a virtue but involvement is a peril; freedom demands cruelty. The world comprehends instinctively that the artist, the fanatic, the lover of beauty, the anarchist are its enemies. Thus it must work to control, to pervert, to tame, and to castrate what it senses to be its enemy. *The Glass Menagerie* understates these discoveries, paralleling the covert way in which life itself reveals them.

—Nancy M. Tischler, "The Distorted Mirror: Tennessee Williams' Self-Portraits," *Mississippi Quarterly* 25, no. 3 (Fall 1972): 389–403.

[James Hafley is the author of *The Glass Roof: Virginia Woolf as Novelist*. In this excerpt Hafley posits that light and youth, Williams's favorite abstractions, are ambivalent and illusory terms in his works.]

Williams' favorite abstracts seem to be *light* (regularly "fading" or "dimming"), *love, reverence, blue* and the constantly recurring *youth. Light* is most often related to imagery of glass, from Laura's animals to a profusion of mirrors to the ice of *Moise.* Glass exhibits the favored ambivalence: it can reveal, or seem to, what is beyond, or it can reflect what is only before it; it can tell truth, but is the most fragile of substances; like smoke it hovers as image between the concrete and the abstract: next to invisible, yet with a visibility that must ultimately damn it into mortality. For in Williams' world knowledge has only negative value when pitted against the lunatic falsehood of justifying fancy. The light as it dims, as it fades, proves the glass to be literal glass only.

Light can be either a concrete or an abstract noun; even more so *youth,* which as word and image (object) is central in this art. *Youth* is at once the most attractive abstract and the most transitory concrete: what's soonest lost but most needs finding, soonest faded but most deserves perduration. The poem "Testa Dell' Effebo"—"Testa" both real and simulated—is a convenient example of the paradox of youth as both lost and saved: as real in life but ideal in art. The sculpture of that poem is analogous to the word *youth* (art) as opposed to the condition of youth (life). The sculpture, the word, are at once involved with life and safe from it: art is a solution infinitely preferable to lunacy. Art allows comedy as lunacy demands tragedy (here mortality). In this poem the language dramatizes the word become Word (compare Hart Crane's *Voyages*). The real youth after his youth has ended, dimmed, must have become lunatic; the youth in art remains youth to time present—"this" time—and indeed prompts the language of life in this speech of praise. He has progressed from Flora to copper, but the speech reenacts his past most comfortably, and the copper cast exhibits, eternalizes, the "luster" and "repose" (the only two abstract words in the poem), hence realizing the ideal as it idealizes the real in a turning of change to permanence. Indeed, the last line suggests both that the sculpture has immortalized the youth and that he has shed his mortality, cast it off in pure ideality. The ancillary imagery here of eyes, glasses, birds, typically marks the youth's turning from seeming to genuine permanence. Like the marvelous children of "In Jack-O-Lantern's Weather" he exists "north of time:" located beyond location.

But art itself is subject to decay, as the mere thought of *The Glass Menagerie* insists. If a zoo of Kowalskis can be tamed into glass, its fixity is transparent in both senses. And if the obligingly mediating glass cannot only idealize the real but also realize the ideal, the unicorn, that realization is almost certainly a betrayal into the merely ordinary, the horse. Glass is for Williams a grand correlative for abstraction as ideal: a meeting ground where the miracle occurs but, occurring, subjects itself to time and hence to destruction. As the copper of "Testa" permitted the comic *ars longa* (art endures), so, and much oftener, the glass announces *vita brevis ars brevisque* (both life and art soon perish). Like Laura's unicorn the abstractions of *Menagerie* are shattered by the concretes, just as time present in that play is mere illusion, and time past (the same thing) only a memory.

—James Hafley, "Abstraction and Order in the Language of Tennessee Williams," *Tennessee Williams: A Tribute*, ed. Jac Tharpe (Jackson: University of Mississippi Press, 1977): 753–762.

ESTHER MERLE JACKSON ON THE HAMLET DEVICE AND THE ANTI-HERO

[Esther Merle Jackson is the author of *The Broken World of Tennessee Williams* (1965). In this excerpt, she notes the similarities between Tom and Shakespeare's Hamlet as models of the conscious self; here as a reflection of twentieth-century man.]

A subtle use of the Hamlet device may be seen in *The Glass Menagerie*. For Williams creates in this drama a conscious self: the observing and reflecting "Tom" who projects the flow of experience from his own recall. Within his stream of consciousness there exists another "Tom," the acting self. As the play progresses, it becomes evident that each of the other members of Tom's family represents a position in his pattern of understanding. *The Glass Menagerie,* like O'Neill's *The Great God Brown,* is an exploration of life possibilities, a review of the roles conceived by an anti-heroic man. In *The Glass Menagerie* Williams conceives three of these masks: that of Amanda, the self of natural life; of Laura, the self of poetry and illusion; and of the father, the self of action. Tom explains his choice of a life role in these words,

> I didn't go to the moon, I went much further—for time is the longest distance between two places—. . . .

> I left Saint Louis. I descended the steps of this fire-escape for a last time and followed, from then on, in my father's footsteps. . . .

In *The Glass Menagerie,* as in the other major works of Tennessee Williams, the protagonist pursues his "odyssey," his journey toward selfhood. Within the "lyric instant," the moment of escape from the corrosive life process, the protagonist conducts his search for a principle through which he may bring meaning to experience. He does this by exploring the alternatives mirrored within this image of his own consciousness. Williams thus examines a comprehensive theme of twentieth-century arts, the search for identity: the journey toward meaning. It is because of his perception of a moral crisis that Williams has abandoned more flattering images of man. Apparently shocked and frightened by the growing threat of human annihilation, he suggests that the theatre cannot afford to exalt man, to praise and to commend his nature. He insists that the proper function of the modern drama is to expose man's hidden nature, to search out his motives, to discover his limits, and, ultimately, to help him to find a mode of salvation. There is little doubt that in his anti-hero Williams states the case against modern man effectively. However, he has been able to evolve only a limited resolution for his cycle of suffering. He concludes that the only hope for man is compassion. It is love that redeems the damned city of Camino Real and sets the "water to flowing again in the mountains."

The anti-heroic protagonist of Williams is designed to reveal the nature of suffering as it appears in the life of the twentieth century. He is intended as the object of pity and terror in the modern world. A question is often asked about this aspect of Williams' work: Of what meaning is the fate of his emotional, spiritual, and moral cripples? The answer given by Williams reflects the gradual usurpation of the pagan idea of tragedy by the Christian concept of human worth. For the Christian ethic holds every man a sinner, redeemable only through love. Similarly, it insists, as does Williams, that all men are anti-heroic; that these figures, no more than others, are guilty of the human condition. In this context, Williams' catalogue of transgressors in search of salvation is a true symbolism—his anti-hero, the very present image of man.

—Esther Merle Jackson, "The Anti-Hero in the Plays of Tennessee Williams" (editor's title), in *The Broken World of Tennessee Williams* (Madison: University of Wisconsin Press, 1965). Reprinted in *Tennessee Williams: A Collection of Critical Essays*, ed. Stephen S. Stanton (Englewood Cliffs, NJ: Prentice-Hall, 1977): 97–99.

ROGER B. STEIN ON ILLUSION AND FRUSTRATION

[Roger B. Stein is the author of *John Ruskin and Aesthetic Thought in America, 1840–1900* and *Seascape and the American Imagination*. In this excerpt Stein discusses the social ironies and personal frustrations that shape the progress of the characters in *The Glass Menagerie*.]

What holds the play together are Tom's remembrances of things past, not plot or characterization. Tom, the poet-narrator and author's surrogate, called "Shakespeare" in the warehouse, organizes the drama symbolically through language and image. This is the "new plastic theatre" of which Williams spoke in his production notes, a revelation not through dramatic struggle but through the allusive power of the word, the accretion of symbolic clusters which bear the meaning, reinforced dramaturgically through lighting, music, the distancing devices of a narrator and, as originally planned, of screen images.

The glass menagerie is itself the most obvious organizing symbol. It embodies the fragility of Laura's world, her search for beauty; it registers sensitively changes in lighting and stand in vivid contrast to the harshness of the outer world which can (and does) shatter it so easily. The unicorn can become the gift to Jim the

Gentleman Caller, whose anticipation and appearance form the plot of the play, only when it has lost its mythical uniqueness, the horn, when dream becomes momentarily possibility before it is obliterated at the end. The magic of Prince Charming's kiss cannot work ("Stumblejohn," he brands himself in the published version of the play, taking on for the moment Laura's crippled condition). The "little silver slipper of a moon" on which Amanda has asked Laura to wish becomes an ironic image of Laura's isolated condition, but Amanda, wrapped up in her own illusions and selling magazine subscriptions and brassieres (like the "Gay Deceivers" with which she tries to stuff Laura before Jim appears) prefers to believe not in Tom's favorite D. H. Lawrence, but in Cinderella and courtly love and *Gone With the Wind*, the novel to which she compares Bessie May Harper's latest effort in *The Homemaker's Companion*. The ironies of the allusive imagery proliferate: Amanda's heroic efforts as homemaker are unsuccessful (the father appears only as a happy doughboy photographic image), and Margaret Mitchell's depression romance about the desirable Scarlett O'Hara in a lost Eden, a South fantasized in the national imagination during the Depression, only makes Laura look more forlorn. Finally one may note that the title image itself of *Gone With the Wind* underlines the evanescent quality of this dream and all of the Wingfields' illusions. As such, it points directly to the last line of the play and Tom's injunction to "Blow out your candles, Laura."

On the level of plot, this widening circle of reference enhances the credibility of the dramatic situation. Given Amanda's sham version of idealized love and a fantasy past, how could the Gentleman Caller's visit be other than a failure? Despite Amanda's dress which is "historical almost," despite the attempt to live in the nineteenth century when the electric power goes off, Jim is not Rhett Butler but an "emissary from a world of reality," as Tom calls him, an engaged twentieth-century man on vacation. The flickering candlelight of Jim's scene with Laura is not enough to sustain the illusion; at the end of their scene this illusion collapses and we are left in darkness.

But *The Glass Menagerie* is built upon more than the poignant plot of illusion and frustration in the lives of little people. Williams has deepened the losses of individuals by pointing to social and even spiritual catastrophe. The time of the play is

1939, as the narrative frame makes explicit both at the beginning and the end. The life of illusion is not confined to the Wingfields alone. As Tom says, "the huge middle class of America was matriculating in a school for the blind." What he calls the "social background" of the play has an important role. The international backdrop is Guernica and the song America sings is "The World is Waiting for the Sunrise," for the sober truth is that America is still in the depression and on the brink of war. The note of social disaster runs throughout the drama, fixing the lives of individuals against the larger canvas.

Amanda's anxieties are in large part economic and there is money behind many of her illusions: her mythical suitors were all wealthy men, as are her magazine heroes; she computes the money Tom would save by giving up smoking. When Tom complains of the grimness of life in the shoe factory, she replies, "Try and you will SUCCEED!" If this is another of Amanda's illusions, it is one shared by her fellow Americans, for "try and you will succeed" is the traditional motto of the American dream of success, the theme of confident self-reliance canonized in the romances of Horatio Alger.

It is not Amanda, however, but Jim, the emissary from reality, who is the chief spokesman for the American dream. To Jim the warehouse is not a prison but a rung on the ladder toward success. He believes in self-improvement through education, and the lecture on self-confidence which he reads to Laura is part of the equipment of the future executive. He is awed by the fortune made in chewing gum and rhapsodizes on the theme of the future material progress of America: "All that remains is for the industry to get itself under way! Full steam— *Knowledge— Zzzzp! Money— Zzzzp! Power!* That's the cycle democracy is built on!"

Yet when the theme of success is superimposed upon the lives of the characters, the social irony emerges. Father was not the successful businessman, but a telephone man who "fell in love with long distance." Tom, the substitute father, refuses to pay the light bill, plunges his family into darkness, and then runs out, and Amanda sells subscriptions and brassieres only at the loss of her dignity. Jim's own dream of success seems to have reached its peak in high school. (Williams later explored this theme more fully in *Cat on a Hot Tin Roof.*) The trek upward through the depression years is disappointing, but the indomitable optimist is not discouraged.

—Roger B. Stein, "*The Glass Menagerie* Revisited: Catastrophe without Violence," *Western Humanities Review* 18 (Spring 1964): 141–153.

C. W. E. Bigsby on a Certain Courage

[C. W. E. Bigsby is Reader in American Literature in the School of English and American Studies at the University of East Anglia. His works include *Dada and Surrealism, Confrontation and Commitment: A Study of Contemporary American Drama, 1959–1966* and studies of Tom Stoppard, Joe Orton, and Edward Albee. Here Bigsby probes Williams's nostalgic reconstruction of an illusory past.]

What he celebrates in *The Glass Menagerie* is a certain courage ("the most magnificent thing in all human nature is valor—and endurance," he once remarked) and, finally, a compassion that wins out over self-interest, despair and cruelty. Thus he tells us in a stage direction at the end of the play that "the interior scene is played as though viewed through soundproof glass. Amanda appears to be making a comforting speech to Laura who is huddled upon the sofa. Now that we cannot hear the mother's voice, her silliness is gone and she has dignity and tragic beauty. Laura's dark hair hides her face until at the end of the speech she lifts it to smile at her mother." *The Glass Menagerie* was an attempt to lay the ghosts of his own past. It was a play which he, like his protagonist, had to write and it was not for nothing that he gave his poet his own name. It was also a play which, in its elegiac tone, dramatised his problematic relationship to the past—personal and cultural. And the past has always been a major concern of the Southern writer.

The South that Williams pictures is either disintegrating, its moral foundations having been disturbed, or being taken over by the alienated products of modern capitalism. On the one hand are the rich, cancerous, their economic power signalled, in Lawrencian manner, through sexual impotence as in *Orpheus Descending*, or incestuous passion as in *Suddenly Last Summer* and *Sweet Bird of Youth*; on the other hand are the new, brutal proletariat, as in *A Streetcar Named Desire*, who begin by destroying a South become decadent and end, in *The Red Devil Battery Sign*, by destroying even themselves. It is a Spenglerian vision. Williams's sensibility was in an almost permanent state of recoil. The collapse of the South, though by no means unambiguous, is in some ways seen as the collapse of culture. The process is irresistible. What interests Williams is how the individual will negotiate a temporary reprieve from the progress of history and time. The uncoiling of the spring of history deconstructs the grace of youth, attenuates the urgent, authentic passions and subtle illusions with which the individual and state alike began. His characters exist in a world "sick with neon," in which pastel shades have for the most part deferred to primary colours, the wistful music of Laura's theme (in *The Glass Menagerie*) or the Vasouviana (in *Streetcar*) being superseded by the rhythms of the dance-hall band. And that music forges a link between Miller and Williams, who both locate their characters in the same no-man's-land, stranded between the real and the imagined, the spiritual and the material, a discordant present and a lyric nostalgia. Hence the flute music heard in *Death of a Salesman* is described by Miller as recalling "grass, and trees and the horizon," a lost world of lyricism and beauty confused with sadness, while the distant music of *The Glass Menagerie* is intended by Williams as "the lightest, most delicate music in the world and perhaps the saddest." It is "like circus music," heard "not when you are on the grounds or in the immediate vicinity of the parade, but when you are at some distance and very likely thinking of something else. . . . It expresses the surface vivacity of life with the underlying strain of innumerable and inexpressible sorrows." "Nostalgia," he suggests, "is the first condition of the play," as it is in a sense of all Williams's work, but it is a nostalgia for a past which he could not entirely convince himself had ever existed.

—C. W. E. Bigsby, "Celebration of a Certain Courage," *A Critical Introduction to Twentieth Century American Drama*, vol. 2, *Tennessee Williams, Arthur Miller, Edward Albee* (Cambridge University Press, 1984). Reprinted in *Modern Critical Interpretations: The Glass Menagerie*, ed. Harold Bloom (New York: Chelsea House, 1988): 89–91.

[Eric P. Levy is author of *Metaphysical Shock: A Study of the Novels of Bernard Malamud.* In this excerpt Levy probes the way in which Amanda's words shape Laura's perception of herself in the mirror.]

In his production notes introducing *The Glass Menagerie,* Tennessee Williams refers to nostalgia as "the first condition of the play." This appraisal at first seems accurate, for the drama disposes the past in a series of receding planes by which the very notion of nostalgia is progressively deepened. From the perspective of Tom, the narrator and a chief character, the past when he started "to boil inside" with the urge to leave home becomes a haunting memory from which his present struggles vainly to flee. But the confining power of that past derives from his mother's nostalgic attachment to her own more distant past and the desperate need to exploit motherhood as a means of reviving "*the legend of her youth.*"

Yet once we analyze how Amanda manipulates maternity, a factor in the play more fundamental than nostalgia will begin to emerge. This principle is self-consciousness—a term which, as we shall see, the text supplies and in its own way defines. Each character is hampered in relating to others by the need to inhabit a private world where the fundamental concern is with self-image. Some characters (Amanda and Jim) use others as mirrors to reflect the self-image with which they themselves wish to identify. Other characters (Laura and Tom) fear that through relation to others they will be reduced to mere reflections, trapped in the mirror of the other's judgment. In virtue of this preoccupation with self-image and the psychological mirrors sustaining it, the world of the play is aptly named after glass. Indeed, Laura's remark ironically becomes the motto of the play: "My glass collection takes up a good deal of time. Glass is something you have to take good care of."

Let us begin be examining Amanda's influence on Laura. Unwittingly, Amanda exploits her maternal concern about Laura's lack of marital prospects as a means of identifying with her own past when she herself was visited one Sunday afternoon in Blue Mountain by "seventeen!—gentlemen callers." In effect, she turns her daughter into a mirror in which her own flattering self-image is reflected, but to do so she must first turn herself or, more precisely, her parental judgment, into a mirror reflecting Laura's limitations. The play itself suggests this seminal image. After helping Laura dress and groom herself, Amanda instructs her to stand in front of a real mirror: "Now look at yourself, young lady. This is the prettiest you will ever be! . . . I've got to fix myself now! You're going to be surprised by your mother's appearance!" Then "*Laura moves slowly to the long mirror and stares solemnly at herself.*"

Look closely at what is happening here. Amanda slights Laura's appearance even as she praises it. Laura is told that she has reached her peak at this moment: she will never again be as attractive. But Laura's limitation only enhances Amanda's excitement about her own "spectacular appearance!" The literal mirror in which Laura beholds her own image ultimately symbolizes her mother's judgment of her. Yet the fundamental purpose of that judgment is to provide, by contrast, a flattering self-image for Amanda. Though on this occasion Amanda's judgment seems benign, it participates in a subtle pattern of comparison by which Laura is made to identify with the sense of her own "Inferiority" to her mother. Indeed, at one point she alludes explicitly to this fact: "I'm just not popular like you were in Blue Mountain." Laura is, in her own words, "crippled." But her primary handicap concerns, not the limp caused by a slight inequality in the length of her legs, but the negative self-consciousness instilled by her mother. In fact Jim, the gentleman caller, approaches this very diagnosis. When Laura recalls how in high school she "had to go clumping all the way up the aisle with everyone watching," Jim advises: "You shouldn't have been self-conscious."

The effect of Laura's self-consciousness is to make her intensely protective of her self-image and to shield it from exposure to anyone outside the home. Whenever she is forced to interact or perform in public, she becomes suddenly ill with nausea and must withdraw. The most extreme example of this syndrome is her brief attendance at Rubicam's Business College where, according to the typing instructor, Laura "broke down completely—was sick at the stomach and almost had to be carried into the wash room." She has a similar reaction after the arrival of Jim at the Wingfield home, and reclines alone on her couch while the others dine in another room. As a result of this withdrawal reflex, Laura has no life outside preoccupation with her own vulnerability.

But paradoxically, the very intensity of this preoccupation changes the meaning of the vulnerability it concerns. By focusing on the fear of humiliating exposure, Laura eventually identifies, not with the shame evoked by her self-image, but with the desperate need to avoid suffering it. In this context, the playwright's commentary on Laura gains greater profundity: "Laura's separation increases till she is like a piece of her own glass collection, too exquisitely fragile to move from the shelf." At bottom, the purpose of Laura's withdrawal *is* to heighten her "fragility;" for, through belief in the damaging effect of exposure, she exchanges a negative self-image for one more flattering. Sensitivity to shame allows Laura to identify with her worthiness, not of ridicule, but of delicate care and compassion. Yet instead of leading to "confidence," this escape from shame depends on increasing her insecurity. She is safe from exposure to shame only if she identifies with her inability to endure it. But lack of confidence is Laura's secret wish, or it protects from confronting anything more threatening in life than her own familiar anxiety. Indeed, whenever she is encouraged to go beyond this anxiety, her reflex is to pick up on of her "little glass ornaments." She does this when Amanda reminds her of the need for eventual marriage and during the conversation with Jim.

—Eric P. Levy, "'Through Soundproof Glass': The Prison of Self-Consciousness in *The Glass Menagerie*," *Modern Drama* 36, no. 4 (December 1993): 529–531.

JACQUELINE O'CONNOR ON CONFINEMENT AND ISOLATION IN *MENAGERIE*

[Jacqueline O'Connor is assistant professor of English at Stephen F. Austin State University where she teaches drama, American literature, and composition. She has published articles on David Rabe, Anna Cora Mowatt, and Tennessee Williams. In this selection O'Connor discusses how the play's set constructs the sense of both physical and psychological confinement.]

Many of Williams's plays take place in confined space, and the setting often suggests that the characters will face permanent confinement at the play's end. *The Glass Menagerie* is set in "one of those hive-like conglomerations of cellular living-units . . . symptomatic of the impulse of this largest and fundamentally enslaved section of American society to avoid fluidity and differentiation." Confinement figures as a major theme in this drama; Tom speaks frequently about the confinement that keeps him from fulfilling his dreams. In scene three, he berates his mother for the lack of privacy he feels in the apartment, telling her: "I've got no thing, no single thing—in my life that I can call my own!" He feels confined in his job, sarcastically wondering if Amanda thinks he wants to spend "fifty-five *years* down there in that—*celotex interior!* with—*fluorescent— tubes!*" When he returns from a night out, he brags to Laura about the magician who performed the coffin trick: "We nailed him into a coffin and he got out of the coffin without removing one nail." This, he claims, constitutes a "trick that would come in handy for me—get me out of this 2x4 situation!" Tom escapes from the oppressive apartment and the dead-end job, but does not find the freedom he expects, for he cannot forget his sister or the ties he feels to her, which bind him even in her absence.

Laura is voluntarily confined in the apartment, which, according to her mother, will lead to permanent confinement if she does not pursue a career or marriage. She will end up one of those "barely tolerated spinsters . . . stuck away in some little mouse-trap of a room." To the audience Laura's plight seems as constricted as the future her mother predicts, but if Laura's life proceeds as Lucretia's and Blanche's do, the "mouse-trap of a room" might well be in the state asylum. As Tom realizes, Laura is not just crippled: "In the eyes of others—strangers—she's terribly shy and lives in a world of her own and those things make her seem a little peculiar to people outside the house." Amanda's comment highlights Laura's social shortcomings, while Tom's remark focuses on her psychological ones: both assessments emphasize Laura's isolation.

—Jacqueline O'Connor, *Dramatizing Dementia: Madness in the Plays of Tennessee Williams* (Bowling Green, OH: Bowling Green State University Popular Press, 1997): 20.

Plot Summary of
A Streetcar Named Desire

Blanche DuBois, in *A Streetcar Named Desire*, is what critic Ruby Cohn calls Williams's "masterpiece of contradiction." Blanche visits the New Orleans home of her sister, Stella, and her brother-in-law, Stanley Kowalski. She is horrified by the contrast between the Kowalski's squalid surroundings in the tenement called "Elysian fields," and her idealized, dreamlike memory of life at Belle Reve (Beautiful Dream), the family estate lost through bankruptcy. During most of the play's 11 scenes Blanche plays the role of the southern lady, avoiding the subject of her own "epic fornications," which were somehow responsible for the foreclosure on Belle Reve (**scenes one** and **two**). She tells Stella that she has suffered a nervous breakdown. Stella realizes that Blanche and Stanley will not get along and tries to prepare her sister before her husband arrives, but Stanley's crude humor and animal maleness offend her. Stanley bitterly resents Blanche's affected refinement and her intrusion into his sexual privacy with Stella. Blanche is well-read and educated, her speech distinguished from the Kowalskis by her vocabulary and cultural references, but her comments are trite and often incongruous, as in her later professed hope that Stella's baby will have eyes "like two blue candles lighted in a white cake."

Blanche soaks in the bathtub (**scene two**): Stella plans to take her out for the evening so she will not interfere with Stanley's poker night. She tries to calm Stanley about the loss of Belle Reve which, he feels, is his loss as much as Stella's. He thinks Blanche has squandered the proceeds. Whether or not she believes Blanche's story Stella defends her sister. When Blanche emerges from the bathroom Stanley is waiting for her. She flirts, even sprays him with cologne, until Stanley confronts her about Belle Reve. He looks for the papers regarding the foreclosure in her trunk and finds instead a packet of love letters written by her late husband, Allan. She vows to burn the letters because Stanley has touched them. In many ways Blanche's fate is equivalent to a classic tragedy: Her downfall, against which she struggles mightily, seems undeserved, but unavoidable.

Stanley holds a poker party at which Blanche meets Mitch (**scene three**) whom she thinks is as lonely and as "superior to the others" as she. Acting the part of the southern belle she tells him "I can't stand a naked lightbulb any more than I can a rude remark or a vulgar action." She thinks that she might marry him; that he might be a refuge from the past, "a cleft in the rock of the world that I could hide in." Blanche has already tried to escape her past, which she calls "an old tin can [on] the tail of a kite;" she tries to escape the present through liquor and self-delusions about her age, beauty, and former admirers. The climax of the play builds after Blanche asserts that Stella's marriage and unborn child are products of a lust as aimless as the "street-car named Desire" that moves through the narrow streets of New Orleans: She implores Stella to resist the future with Stanley and his kind, and not to "hang back with the brutes (**scene four**)." Stanley has overheard their conversation and Stella seems now poised at a crossroads in this symbolic clash between the civilization that Blanche parodies and the barbarism to which Stanley seems a throwback.

In **scene five** Stanley reveals that he has met a man from Laurel who remembers having met a whore named Blanche at a seedy hotel there. Blanche denies it, but her nervousness proves it to be true. Later, she asks Stella for advice on how intimate she can become with Mitch, who is coming to take her out that evening, without losing his respect. The moment is both comic and tragic. Soon after Stella and Stanley leave for the evening a high school boy comes to collect for the newspaper. Blanche kisses him, afterward muttering "It would be nice to keep you, but I've got to be good and keep my hands off children." Moments later Mitch arrives with roses for her (**scene six**). Although Blanche mocks Mitch's simple, buffoon-like admiration, marriage is on both their minds. She tells him the story of her marriage, a tale of love, violence, and homosexuality that moves him to tears. When Mitch reveals his tender feelings for his dying mother Blanche is moved to confess her promiscuities: "After the death of Allan intimacies with strangers was all I seemed able to fill my empty heart with." Mitch realizes that Blanche is as lonely as he and kisses her.

Later Stanley tells Stella that he has revealed to Mitch that Blanche lost her schoolteaching job and was driven out of town for seducing a 17-year-old student in a hotel (**scene seven**). Stanley gives Blanche a bus ticket home to Laurel, the site of her humiliation. As **scene eight** ends, Stella goes into labor and the couple rush to the hospital. Mitch arrives later that evening (**scene nine**) and confronts Blanche with the scandal Stanley has revealed. Though she has been drinking heavily, Blanche attempts to sustain the role of the lady. Mitch feels betrayed by her and demands that she give to him what she has withheld all summer—her body. She says she will if only he'll marry her, but Mitch declares her not clean enough to inhabit the same house as his mother.

Stanley returns in **scene ten**. The baby has not come yet and he will spend the night at home. After they exchange some dangerous, sexually charged banter Blanche infuriates Stanley when she tells him that she has put Mitch in his place for his cruelty to her. He threatens her and she breaks a bottle on the edge of the table, intending to defend herself, but Stanley nevertheless rapes her. Stella returns from the hospital with her baby and Blanche tells her what happened (**scene eleven**). Stella confides to Eunice "I couldn't believe her story and go on living with Stanley." Eunice agrees, "Don't ever believe it. Life has got to go on. No matter what happens, you've got to keep on going." Stella prefers to believe that Blanche is in the grip of a psychotic fantasy and has her committed to a mental institution. Blanche, helpless and defeated, leaves with the doctor and the attendants, saying only, "Whoever you are I have always depended on the kindness of strangers." Stella never accepts the fact that the rape occurred and, after Blanche is taken away, she and Stanley resume their almost wordless animal intimacy. ❀

List of Characters in
A Streetcar Named Desire

Blanche DuBois is an English teacher who has recently lost her job because, as the superintendent's letter describes it, she was "morally unfit for her position." Like Amanda Wingfield in *A Glass Menagerie* she tempers her loneliness and despair with illusions about the past and the future. She comes to stay at "Elysian Fields," in New Orleans, in the tenement apartment of her younger sister, Stella, and her brother-in-law, Stanley Kowalski. The family estate, Belle Reve, has been sold in foreclosure and her homosexual husband has committed suicide, an event that seems to have driven her to sexual excesses that enraged her neighbors enough to throw her out of Laurel, Mississippi. Always charming, ladylike, and flirtatious, Blanche has an air of superiority and affectation that enrages Stanley. Although Blanche's actions and lies make her an object of derision, her past behavior may be indeed defensible. Her beauty, property, career, and ultimately, her sanity leave her. After Stanley rapes her she is taken away to the asylum.

Stanley Kowalski is a plainspoken, often brutal man who hates pretension and affectation. He is unimpressed with Blanche's education and refinement, except as it infuriates him. Drinking, bowling, and poker are surpassed only by sex among his favorite activities. He hits Stella, shouts, throws dishes, tosses the radio out the window, and brutally rapes Blanche. Though many critics and playgoers have found him charming (especially in Marlon Brando's portrayal), his malice toward Blanche is difficult to justify. Is he merely an animal defending his territory against an intruder? Blanche's presence interferes with his sex life with Stella, and she attempts to turn Stella against her "brute" husband. When Stanley discovers the truth about Blanche's past, he feels free to destroy her in the most direct and unpretentious manner he knows.

Stella Kowalski seems an unlikely wife for Stanley. She endures both Stanley's tantrums and her sister's criticisms with equal aplomb. What Stella and Stanley seem to share is an interest in their sex life together and bowling. When Blanche tells her about the rape Stella believes only that her sister is delusional and commits her to an asylum. Like Blanche, she would rather believe the illusion than the unpleasant reality.

Harold ("Mitch") Mitchell is a dull and ordinary man, but Blanche realizes the limits of her romantic prospects and is ready to consider marriage to him. He is polite to Blanche, unmarried, and the first man to treat her like a lady since her arrival. He, in turn, is looking for someone as gentle and refined as Blanche appears to be. His mother, he thinks, would approve. Stanley reveals the truth of Blanche's past to Mitch and the relationship ends.

Eunice Hubbell and her husband, Steve, live upstairs. She pries, either in a nosy or a sisterly way, depending upon your perspective, into the lives of the Kowalskis. About Stanley's rape of Blanche she advises Stella, "Don't ever believe it. Life has got to go on. No matter what happens, you've got to keep on going." There is no other way, in her thinking, to come to terms with the vulgarity that surrounds them all.

Steve Hubbell plays poker and drinks with Stanley. He is as crude and prone to violence as Stanley.

Pablo Gonzales is the fourth member of Stanley's regular card-playing group.

Blanche meets a **young collector** when he comes to collect for the newspaper. She kisses him instead of paying him, reminding us of her past seductions and of her dead husband.

The **nurse** and **doctor** come to the apartment to take Blanche to the asylum. As the nurse prepares to put Blanche into a straight-jacket, the doctor intervenes and assumes a more gentle approach. Blanche gratefully thanks him. ❈

Critical Views of
A Streetcar Named Desire

JOHN GASSNER ON THE SOCIAL BASE OF PRIVATE DRAMA

[John Gassner (1903–1967) published widely on American theater. His works include *Theatre at the Crossroads: Plays and Playwrights of the Mid-Century American Stage* and *Dramatic Soundings.* In this selection Gassner analyzes Blanche's impossible social position and her place as a symbol of a decadent Southern aristocracy.]

In *A Streetcar Named Desire,* health and disease are at odds with each other, but here the dialectical situation flares up into relentless conflict. The lines are sharply drawn in this more naturalistic drama, whose story, unlike that of *The Glass Menagerie,* is no longer revealed impressionistically through the merciful mist of memory. Nothing is circuitous in *A Streetcar,* and the dramatic action drives directly to its fateful conclusion as plebeian and patrician confront each other. Like other southern heroines of Williams, who invariably suggest Picasso's dehydrated "Demoiselles d'Avignon," Blanche DuBois is not only a recognizable human being but an abstraction— the abstraction of decadent aristocracy as the painter's inner eye sees it. It is her final tragedy that the life she encounters in a married sister's home cannot spare her precisely when she requires the most commiseration. Her plantation lost, the teaching profession closed to her, her reputation gone, her nerves stretched to the snapping-point, Blanche has come to Stella in the French Quarter to find her married to a lusty ex-sergeant of Polish extraction. She is delivered into his untender hands when he discovers her lurid past and, although he may be momentarily touched by her fate on learning of the unhappy marriage that drove her to moral turpitude, his standards do not call for charity. With her superior airs and queasiness she has interfered with Stanley's married happiness, and she must go. Loyal to his friend, who served in the same military outfit with him, he must forewarn Mitch, who is about to propose to her, that the southern lady has been a harlot, thus destroying her last hope. Having sensed a challenge to his robust manhood from the moment he met Blanche, he must even violate her. It is his terrible health, which is of earth and will defend itself at any cost, that destroys

Blanche, and sister Stella herself must send the hapless woman to a state institution if she is to protect her marriage and preserve her faith in Stanley.

As in *The Glass Menagerie* and in the one-acters, the private drama is pyramided on a social base. Blanche is the last descendant to cling to the family plantation of Belle Reve, sold acre by acre by improvident male relatives "for their epic fornications, to put it plainly," as she says. Her simple-hearted sister declassed herself easily by an earthy marriage to Stanley Kowalski and saved herself. Blanche tried to stand firm on quicksand and was declassed right into a house of ill-fame. The substructure of the story has some resemblance to *The Cherry Orchard*, whose aristocrats were also unable to adjust to reality and were crushed by it. Nevertheless, Williams subordinated his oblation to reality, his realization that Stanley and the denizens of the New Orleans slum street called Elysian Fields represent health and survival, to a poet's pity for Blanche. For him she is not only an individual whose case must be treated individually but a symbol of the many shorn lambs for whom no wind is ever tempered except by the godhead in men's hearts and the understanding of artists like Williams himself. It is surely for this reason that the author called his play a "tragedy of incomprehension" and "entered," in the words of his quotation from Hart Crane, "the broken world to trace the visionary company of love, its voice an instant in the wind (I know not whither hurled)." It is in the light of this compassion that the pulse of the play becomes a succession of musical notes and the naturalism of the writing flares into memorable lines, as when Blanche, finding herself loved by Mitch, sobs out, "Sometimes there's God so quickly."

As his plays multiply, it will be possible to measure him against dramatists whom his writing so often recalls—against Chekhov, Gorki, O'Neill, and Lorca. That such comparisons can be even remotely envisioned for an American playwright under thirty-five is in itself an indication of the magic of his pen; and it will soon be seen whether this magic works in *Summer and Smoke*, another, but more complicated, southern drama which carries a woman's soul to Tartarus. The test may prove a severe one, since the new play is episodic enough to be considered a chronicle. Further testing will also gauge the range of his faculties. Williams has himself detected a limitation in the sameness of theme and background in his work. He is turning toward new horizons with two uncompleted plays; one of them is set in Mexico, the other in Renaissance Italy. In time we shall also discover whether he overcomes noticeable inclinations toward a preciosity that could have vitiated *The Glass Menagerie* and toward a melodramatic sensationalism which appears in the rape scene of *A Streetcar Named Desire* and in the addition of wedlock with a homosexual to Blanche's tribulations. All that is beyond question at the present time is that Tennessee Williams is already a considerable artist in a medium in which there are many craftsmen but few artists.

—John Gassner, "Tennessee Williams: Dramatist of Frustration," *College English* 10, no. 10 (October 1948): 1–7.

Signi Falk on Symbolism and Sentimentality, and on Blanch DuBois, Escapist Woman

[Signi Falk is the author of volumes of criticism on the works of Tennessee Williams and Archibald MacLeish. Here Falk discusses Stanley's crude and almost lyrical dissipation. In the second extract Falk describes Blanche as a "glamorized neurotic" in many ways like Williams himself.]

William's most passionately lyrical tribute is bestowed on a type of male animal, a figure worthy of citation at an international stock show. Stan Kowalsky of *A Streetcar Named Desire* has not been spoiled by the American Way of Life: "Animal joy in his being is implicit in all his movements and attitudes. Since early childhood the center of his life has been pleasure with women, the giving and taking of it, not with weak indulgence, dependently, but with power and pride of a richly feathered male bird among hens. . . . He sizes up women with a glance, with sexual satisfactions, crude images flashing into his mind and determining the way he smiles at them." He belongs to Williams' concept of the Elysian Fields, the heaven of poker players, "men at the peak of their physical manhood, as coarse and direct and powerful as primary colors." When Stan, a drunken primitive with a single idea about women, takes the deranged Blanche DuBois, a sentimental prostitute, off to the bedroom and speaks the line, "We've had this date from the beginning!" Williams has arrived theatrically. It is reported that waves of titillated laughter swept over the audience. It was the effect, no doubt, that Williams sought. But it bears no resemblance to the Greek tragedy with which he identifies himself. ⟨. . .⟩

Mitch, another gentleman caller, is Blanche DuBois' last hope in *A Streetcar Named Desire*, a blundering, aging mama's boy. Shocked by his fiancée's past, he throws apron-string ideals out the window and makes a comically ineffective pass at his streetwalker sweetheart. Rosa's sailor in *The Rose Tattoo* is another good boy, a shellback with three equator crossings to his credit but his mother's teachings still in his heart. He is one of Williams' more slightly developed characters, but one of his best, and proof that when he is willing to deliver straightforward, honest writing, rather than indulge in phony symbolism and posturing, he can write with power. [Another] gentleman caller is Roger Doremus in *Summer and Smoke*, more securely mother-attached than either Tom Wingfield or Mitch, a dull young man who drinks lemonade with Alma and waxes enthusiastic about the meeting of his mother and father: "returning from India with dysentery they met on the boat."

⁓

Another escapist, Blanche DuBois, unable to face family deaths and the decay of the state to a "mere twenty acres and a graveyard," turns prostitute in her efforts to find kindness. She is married at sixteen to a young poet, sentimentally described: "Something different about the boy, a nervousness, a softness and a tenderness which wasn't like a man's, although he wasn't effeminate looking." She is widowed shortly afterwards because she discovers this shy boy's relations with an older man. She later becomes an English teacher with rather unusual extracurricular activities: "After the death of Allan—intimacies with strangers was all I seemed able to fill my empty heart with. . . . I think it was panic that drove me from one to another, hunting for some protection—here and there, in the most unlikely places—even, at last, in a seventeen-year-old boy." Strangely enough, she seems surprised that her superintendent should find her "morally unfit for her position." But this may be only Williams' idea of callow American society, too insensitive to understand the exotic and the delicate.

This glamorized neurotic is another of Williams' tragic heroines of the South. Homeless, she descends upon her sister and behaves like an injured grand duchess. She lies about her age, lies about taking liquor, although she has emptied Stan's bottle, lies about her strict ideas of purity though she has been run out of town, turns sexy and exhibitionist before Stan's poker-playing friends, and goes on an emotional drunk with saccharine love songs. She, like her author, insists that she doesn't want realism, but magic. Her condition is deplorable. But the question arises whether she isn't basically another self-centered, dishonest woman, perhaps a nymphomaniac, and whether the writer is not guilty of trying to bewitch his audience with a sentimental portrait of a fraud.

—Signi Falk, "The Profitable World of Tennessee Williams," *Modern Drama* 1, no. 12 (December 1958): 172–180.

ARTHUR GANZ ON STANLEY KOWALSKI AS A LAWRENTIAN LOVER

[Arthur Ganz is the author of *Pinter, a Collection of Critical Essays, Realms of the Self: Variations on a Theme in Modern Drama*, and a critical volume on the works of George Bernard Shaw. In this excerpt Ganz posits that Stanley, as both Blanche's destroyer and the "avenger of her homosexual husband," acts as a symbol of sexual vitality.]

The stage action of *A Streetcar Named Desire*, still Williams' finest play, consists almost entirely of the punishment that its heroine, Blanche DuBois, endures as atonement for her act of rejection, her sin in terms of Williams' morality. Since Williams begins the action of his play at a late point in his story, the act itself is not played out on stage but only referred to. Not realizing that she is describing the crime that condemns her, Blanche tells Mitch of her discovery that her adored young husband was a homosexual and of the consequences of her disgust and revulsion:

BLANCHE: . . . He'd stuck the revolver into his mouth, and fired—
so that the back of his head had been—blown away! (She sways
and covers her face.) It was because—on the dance floor—
unable to stop myself—I'd suddenly said—"I saw! I know! You
disgust me . . ." And then the searchlight which had been turned
on the world was turned off again and never for one moment
since has there been any light that's stronger than this—
kitchen—candle . . .

While Blanche delivers this speech and the ones surrounding it,
the polka to which she and her husband had danced, the Varsouviana, sounds in the background. At the end of the play, when
Blanche sees the doctor who is to lead her off to the asylum, her
punishment is complete and the Varsouviana sounds again, linking
her crime to its retribution. As Blanche flees from the doctor, "the
Varsouviana is filtered into a weird distortion accompanied by the
cries and noises of the jungle." These symbolize simultaneously
Blanche's chaotic state and the instrument of her destruction,
Stanley Kowalski, the complete sensual animal, the equivalent in
function to the black masseur.

Although Kowalski's primary function, to destroy Blanche, is
clear, there are certain ambiguities evoked by his role. By becoming
Blanche's destroyer, Kowalski also becomes the avenger of her
homosexual husband. Although he is Williams' melodramatic
exaggeration of the Lawrentian lover, the embodiment of admired
male sexuality, it is appropriate from Williams' point of view that
Kowalski should to some degree be identified with the lonely
homosexual who had been driven to suicide, for Willliams saw
Lawrence not only as the propagandist of sexual vitality but as the
symbol of the solitary, rejected exile. (See the poem called "Cried
the Fox" from Williams' collection, *In The Winter of Cities*. In it
Lawrence is symbolized as the fox pursued by the cruel hounds.)
By implication, then, Williams has extended Lawrentian approval
to the rejected homosexual (an act that probably set Lawrence
spinning in his grave). Yet this approval is never whole-hearted;
for the exile homosexual, as he appears in Williams' work, is
always tormented and often despairing. He cannot, after all, be a
martyr until Williams has had him crucified.

Those who crucify, however, can never be guiltless. Kowalski,
although an avenger, is as guilty of crucifying Blanche as she is of
crucifying her husband. For Blanche, who has lost the plantation

Belle Reve, the beautiful dream of a life of gracious gentility, is an exile like the homosexual; her tormentor, the apelike Kowalski, from one point of view the representative of Lawrentian vitality, is from another the brutal, male torturer of a lonely spirit. But however compassionately Blanche is viewed, she remains a woman who, in effect, has killed her husband by her cruelty, and her attempts to turn away from death to its opposite—"the opposite is desire," as Blanche herself says—are fruitless. Even as she tells Mitch about her promiscuity, a Mexican woman stands at one side of the stage selling flowers for the dead. "*Flores para los muertos*," she calls, "*flores—flores.*"

—Arthur Ganz, "The Desperate Morality of the Plays of Tennessee Williams," *American Scholar* (Spring 1962): 278–294. Reprinted in *The Chelsea House Library of Literary Criticism: Twentieth-Century American Literature*, vol. 7, ed. Harold Bloom (New York: Chelsea House Publishers, 1988): 4322–4323.

JOSEPH N. RIDDEL ON THE APOLLONIAN-DIONYSIAN MOTIF

[Joseph N. Riddel is the author of *The Turning World: American Literary Modernism and Continental Theory* and *Purloined Letters: Originality and Repetition in American Literature*. In this extract, Riddel examines the tension between Blanche and Stanley as one between self and anti-self.]

The setting of *Streetcar* is a combination of raw realism and deliberate fantasy, a world very much of our society yet timeless and innocent, without ethical dimensions. Williams's evocation of a mythical Elysia suggests a world of the guiltless, of spring and sunlight (though his is shaded, a night world), a pre-Christian paradise where life and passion are one and good. The "Elysian Fields" is New Orleans in several senses: the Elysia where life is pursued on a primitive level beyond or before good and evil. This, I think, must be insisted upon, for the play is a deliberate outrage against conventional morality, a kind of immoralist's protest in the manner if not the style of Gide. The impressionistic scene, lyrical and with an aura of vitality that "attenuates the atmosphere of decay," is a Dionysian world of oneness, where there is an "easy mingling of races" and the pagan chromatics of a "blue piano" provide rhythms for a Bacchic revel.

One does not have to force his interpretation. The humorous vulgarity of the opening section is self-consciously symbolic, abrupt on the level of realism but carefully designed to signify the play's two worlds. Stanley's appearance in his masculine vigor, carrying a "red stained package from the butcher's," competes with the mythical aura of the scene. The implied virility of his gesture in tossing the package to Stella, her suggestive response, and the carefree vigor of their unconcern with time defines succinctly a kind of world that is immediate yet infused with an intensity beyond the real. The scene then pans down on Blanche in her demure and fragile dress, garishly overrefined, overwhelmed by life, out of place in Elysium. She has arrived, we learn, by way of a Freudian streetcar named "Desire," transferring to one called "Cemeteries." The psychoanalytic devices are obvious: Stanley's gesture is vital—prurient yet pure; Blanche on her figurative streetcars has been a pawn of the phallus of desire. If she is a cliché of southern literature, she is likewise the incarnate death wish of civilization. Williams takes his epigraph from Hart Crane's "The Broken Tower," and perhaps also his streetcar from Crane's "For the Marriage of Faustus and Helen," though the poet's work soon jumps its Freudian tracks to become his Faustian artist's symbolic conveyance to a Helen-ideal. Like Crane, Williams finds love in man's "broken world" a "visionary company," an "instant in the wind" suffused with time's desperation. Blanche and Stanley become antiphonal figures in a choric exchange of ideas. The Freudian-Nietzchean paraphernalia operate in close conjunction as a massive assault on the futility of our civilized illusions, which Williams always portrays as both necessary and self-destructive.

The Apollonian-Dionysian motif is vigorously accentuated, but not exactly to Niestzche's purpose. Blanche, as her name implies, is the pallid, lifeless product of her illusions, of a way of life that has forfeited its vigor though what she later calls her family's "epic fornications," perversions of a healthy procreative sex. Her "Belle Reve," the family plantation, rests in Apollo's orchard,

"Laurel," Mississippi. She is in every sense the sum of an exhausted tradition that is the essence of sophistication and culture run down into the appearance that struggles to conceal rapactiy. Her life is a living division of two warring principles, desire and decorum, and she is the victim of civilization's attempt to reconcile the two in a morality. Her indulgent past is a mixture of sin and romance, reality and illusion, the excesses of the self and the restraints of society. Williams has followed Nietzsche in translating what is essentially metaphysical hypothesis into a metaphor of psychological conflict. Her schizoid personality is a drama of man's irreconcilable split between animal reality and moral appearance, or as Freud put it figuratively, a moral conflict of id against ego and superego. Blanche lives in a world of shades, of Chinese lanterns, of romantic melodies that conjure up dream worlds, of perversions turned into illusory romances, of alcoholic escape, of time past—the romantic continuity of generations to which she looks for identity—and of Christian morality that refines away, or judicially and morally vitiates, animal impulse. Thus, she is driven by guilt over the very indulgences that give Stanley's life a vital intensity.

As her antiself, Stanley is as consciously created. Born under the sign of Capricorn, the Goat—as Blanche was born under the sign of Virgo—he is, according to the stage directions, a veritable Pan-Dionysus, the "gaudy seed-bearer," the embodiment of "animal joy" whose life "has been pleasure with women, the giving and taking of it, not with weak indulgence, dependently, but with the power and pride of a richly feathered male bird among hens." He is identified variously with the goat, the cat, and the locomotive, three rather obvious symbols that define his sex-centered life and repeatedly disturb Blanche's tenuous psychic balance. It is revealing, too, that Blanche very early sees in Stanley a source to reinvigorate the DuBois blood. This is no genetic plan but, on Blanche's part, a pathetic hope for the revival of the old dissipated values. She finds her evil lying in the blood and her values in the illusions which can explain away moral indiscretions. Those who acclaimed Williams's earthly inferno mistook the symbolic scene for realism, failing to note the inverted image of a pagan Paradiso, where civilized values are in desuetude and the blood dictates a pulsating order of intensity and calm. The characters are to be judged, if at all, in degree to their response to the rhythm.

The love of Stanley for Stella describes precisely this rhythm of violence and reconciliation, and it exists beyond Blanche's ken. The jazz motif which alternates with the polka music—in contrast to Blanche's affinity for the romantic waltz—establishes the primitive norm to which each character adapts or suffers a dissonant psychic shock. All the old devices are here. The animal appetite is equated with the spiritual appetite for wholeness, and must be satisfied on its own terms, not those of a preestablished ethic. Stanley and Stella move freely between elemental sex and mystical experience, and Williams lends to their relationship every possible symbolic device to enforce the mystical oneness of their union. On the other hand, Blanche's neurotic reveries emerge from the internal drama of conflicting passions caused by her moral conscience. They are to be described, I suppose, in the familiar psychological terms of repression and transference, though the drama seems to lay the cause, not the cure, at the foot of consciousness and reason. Blanche's obsessive bathing is a nominal gesture of guilt and wished-for redemption, which becomes one of the play's recurrent symbols, along with the piano, locomotives, cats, telephones, and drink.

—Joseph N. Riddel, "*A Streetcar Named Desire*—Nietszche Descending," *Modern Drama* 5, no. 4 (February 1963): 21–23.

MARY ANN CORRIGAN ON MUSIC AND THE INELUCTABLE PRIMITIVE FORCES

[Mary Ann Corrigan teaches drama at the University of California, San Diego. In this excerpt Corrigan explores the function of music and Blanche's obsessive bathing in the construction of meaning in the play.]

Music and other sounds communicate a sense of the ineluctable primitive forces that operate in the Vieux Carré. From the Four Deuces, a nearby night spot, come the sounds that express New Orleans life: blues, jazz, honky-tonk. Elia Kazan comments on the function of the "blue piano" music which is in the background of much of the action:

The Blues is an expression of the loneliness and rejection, the exclusion and isolation of the Negro and their longing for love and connection. Blanche, too, is looking for a home, abandoned and friendless. . . . Thus the Blue piano catches the soul of Blanche, the miserable unusual human side of the girl which is beneath her frenetic duplicity, her trickery, lies, etc.

The Blues plays as Blanche arrives in the Vieux Carré and is particularly dominant when she recounts the deaths at Belle Reve and when she kisses the newsboy. As Blanche is being led away to the asylum and Stella cries uncontrollably, the music of the blue piano swells. At one point this music catches the soul of Stanley too: when Stella leaves him, and he sobs, "I want my baby," the "'blue piano' plays for a brief interval." But normally, the uncomplicated obtrusive rhythms of the honky-tonk express Stanley's personality. This music dominates the rape scene.

There is subjective as well as objective music in the play. Only Blanche and the audience hear the Varsouviana polka, which was played as Blanche's husband shot himself. The music, through its association in her memory with impending death, becomes a symbol of imminent disaster. Blanche hears it, for instance, when Stanley hands her a Greyhound bus ticket for a trip back to Laurel. The music of the Varsouviana weaves in and out of the scene in which Mitch confronts Blanche with his knowledge of her background. Williams writes in the stage directions: "*The rapid, feverish polka tune, the 'Varsouviana,' is heard. The music is in her mind; she is drinking to escape it and the sense of disaster closing in on her, and she seems to whisper the words of the song.*" In the same scene the polka tunes fades in as the Mexican street vendor, harbinger of death, arrives, chanting "Flores para los muertos." Reality in all its harshness and ugliness is epitomized for Blanche in these aural and visual reminders of death. She hears this music too in the last scene, when Stanley and the asylum matron corner her. Williams uses the symbolism attaching to Blanche's frequent bathing in order to further lay bare her inner nature. As an aspect of the visiting in-law joke, Blanche's "hogging" of the bathroom is amusing, and the earthy Stanley's references to his bursting kidneys add to the humor. But the serious symbolism is nevertheless obvious: "Blanche's obsessive bathing is a nominal gesture of guilt and wished-for redemption." Like her drinking, her bathing is an escape mechanism. The ritual cleansing which takes place in the tub restores Blanche to a state of former innocence. Once again she is young and pure in a beautiful world

The bath is a particularly functional symbol in scene 7, in which it is used to reveal the dual world of Blanche's existence and the tension between Blanche and Stanley. Stella is setting the table for Blanche's birthday party, to which Mitch, the one person who offers Blanche a genuine possibility for redemption, has been invited. As the scene progresses, it becomes apparent that this birthday will be anything but happy. The festive occasion that falls flat is a staple of drama. Shakespeare, Chekhov, Pinter, and Williams use it to intensify the ironic discrepancy between appearance and reality. As Blanche bathes in preparation for the party, Stanley reveals to Stella the particulars of her sister's sordid life. The stage directions read: "*Blanche is singing in the bathroom a saccharine popular ballad which is used contrapuntally with Stanley's speech.*" The louder Stanley gets in his insistence upon the undeniable facts about Blanche, the louder Blanche sings in the bathroom. Her song asserts the capacity of the imagination to transform mere facts:

> Say, it's only a paper moon. Sailing over a cardboard sea—
> But it wouldn't be make-believe If you believe in me!
>
> . . . .
>
> It's a Barnum and Bailey world. Just as phony as it can be—
> But it wouldn't be make-believe If you believe in me!

When Stanley's recital reaches its climax with the most damning charge of Blanche's seduction of a student, "*in the bathroom the water goes on loud; little breathless cries and peals of laughter are heard as if a child were frolicking in the tub.*" Thus, the two Blanches are counterpoised. In emerging from the bathroom, Blanche immediately senses the threat that Stanley's world of facts poses to her world of illusions. Her usual contented sigh after the bath gives way to uneasiness: "A hot bath and a long, cold drink always give me a brand new outlook on life! . . . Something has happened!—What is it?" Background music reflects her fear: "*The distant piano goes into a hectic breakdown.*"

—Mary Ann Corrigan, "Realism and Theatricalism in *A Streetcar Named Desire*," *Modern Drama* 19, no. 4 (December 1976). Reprinted in *Tennessee Williams's A Streetcar Named Desire*, ed. Harold Bloom (New York: Chelsea House, 1988): 52–53.

[James Hafley is the author of *The Glass Roof: Virginia Woolf as Novelist*. In this excerpt Hafley discusses the interplay of concrete images and abstract ideas in the play.]

Williams' abstractions invariably relate to absolutes, about which he is disarmingly ambivalent: he at once celebrates and shies from transcendence. Thus, the white blackbird and black blackbird of his epigraph to *Moise* exist in a Neoplatonic pattern which is familiar enough; but a tension between conventional longing for the absolute (named by a world of abstract nouns) and individual preference for the spatial/temporal even at its most perilously transitory—this is what is characteristic of Williams. In Williams is neither a sacrificing of real for ideal, nor (as in some Keats or Whitman, say) a total discovery of the ideal in the real; there is dualism and the pull of spirit against flesh, abstraction against concretion, but at the same time a grudge against the very idea of the absolute. His is a world longing for otherness and yet sad or spiteful that such a concept even exists to disturb location in the self; yet self-consciousness defines but also damns by delimitation the identity that it defines.

This ambivalent attitude towards the idea of the ideal is everywhere apparent in Williams' language, where it is dramatized at least as thoroughly as in event. A title like *A Streetcar Named Desire* is apt demonstration. The abstraction "desire"—ranging in its meanings from longing for the absolute to a contradictory lust—is evoked only to be ridiculed as naming a mechanical contrivance, a vulgar corruption of some such conveyance as the ship of life. At the same time, in double irony, the vehicle seems poignantly in need of a magnitude beyond it, like a mailman trying to perform one of the labors of Hercules, or a tenement child named for a king. But the ultimate revelation is of Desire itself as merely a place name, no more in stature or consolation than the streetcar that literally goes there. In the play, Blanche says desire is the opposite of death: it is her conviction prompted by her encounter with the Mexican woman offering flowers for the dead. But she is wrong, and these two grand abstractions, "death" and "desire" ("desire" in Blanche's sense of longing for transcendence) are the same; Stanley's "desire," lust, is the true opponent of death, and the life he gives, like the home he gives, is both pitifully sordid and absolutely necessary to sanity. In this play about homes, Blanche's sublimation of earthy desire that has been denied her leads her from a lost Paradise to a rest home: from innocence to innocence. Stanley's desire and Stella's keep them soundly, vitally located in the experience of time present, in the slum that is the very nutrient of life lived. The situation is not unlike that in Shelley's *Alastor*: humankind can be grateful to the poet, to Blanche, for reaching out to saving ideals; but though the ideal is a model for the salvation of humankind, it is just as surely an illusive alternate to the reality of experienced life. Shelley's speaker, at the end of his account of the idealist poet, cries "O, that the dream . . . were the true law/Of this so lovely world!" In Williams' play, Stella, pulled between the unreal beauty of Blanche's "home" and "desire" and the naked realities of Stanley's, opts for the latter, for law instead of dream—indeed for the legal kinship of her bond to him rather than for her past familial kindness to Blanche. Blanche must rely upon strangers in seeking her kind: sisterhood is a kindness far too real to sustain her elevated sense of home and family, impossibly ideal, impossibly lost. Williams' epigraph from Hart Crane's "the Broken Tower" points to this theme, to "the visionary company" that is a "kindness of strangers," versus the civic family that is a cruelty of kin. *Desire, lost, home*—these words recur tellingly among the play's abstractions. Belle Reve is prelapsarian; the real Elysian Fields is to be found between the L & N tracks and the river.

But major throughout the play are words of relationship (familiarity): *species, type, attachment, kind* and *kindness, companionship*, developing up to Blanche's last speech and giving it its astonishing poetic power and control. In the battle between love and sex, desire and desire, Stanley's crude but real strength, relying on kidneys and not souls, is like the gross earth that alone can nourish belief, imagination, the reaching for the moon which the play defines as "lunacy" in the literal sense of the term. Life is redeemed only by lunatic aspiration, yet it must violate the ideal if only to sustain its desperate knowledge that the L & N tracks are after all not the woodland of Weir. Blanche's name may mean *white*, but her legal name, her married name, is Grey. And all the wonderfully exciting conflicts of this play are first and last conflicts among words, just as the network of conflict I have noticed here is one of battle between concrete and abstract words handled with full awareness of their self-defeating contradictions.

—James Hafley, "Abstraction and Order in the Language of Tennessee Williams," *Tennessee Williams: A Tribute*, ed. Jac Tharpe (Jackson: University Press of Mississippi, 1977): 753–762.

BERT CARDULLO ON BLANCHE DuBOIS AS TRAGIC HEROINE

[Bert Cardullo is the author of *Indelible Images: New Perspectives on Classic Films*, *What Is Dramaturgy?*, *Bazin at Work*, and *The Crommelynck Mystery: The Life and Work of a Belgian Playwright*. Here Cardullo examines evidence of how Blanche's failure to show compassion for her husband brings her destruction.]

As I have observed, those critics of *Streetcar* who dismiss the play outright as tragedy point to the character of Blanche as indisputably that of a clinical case history; they claim that the collapse of her marriage and the death of her homosexual husband made her a victim of neurosis. But they fail to take into account, in Leonard Berkman's words, that "Blanche's most fundamental regret is not that she happened to marry a homosexual," not the *discovery* of Allan's homosexuality (*Stella* believes this). It is that, "when made aware of her husband's homosexuality, she brought on [his] suicide by her unqualified expression of disgust," her *failure* to be compassionate. Confronted in theory with the choice between the expression of compassion and the expression of disgust at the sudden and stunning revelation of Allan's longstanding affair with an older man, she at first "pretended that nothing had been discovered." Then, unable to stop herself, she blurted out abruptly the words of contempt that drove her first and only love to kill himself. I say "confronted in theory with the choice" because, as Blanche herself confesses to Mitch, "[Allan] came to me for help. I didn't know that. . . . All I knew was I'd failed him in some mysterious way and wasn't able to give the help he needed but couldn't speak of! . . . I loved him unendurably but without being able to help him or help myself." Blanche could hardly be expected to respond with love and understanding to her discovery, "in the worst of all possible ways," of Allan's homosexuality (though she struggles to—that is one reason she does not express her disgust immediately), because she had never had a truly intimate, an open and trusting, relationship with him. In the same way, Williams leads us to believe she had never had such a relationship with any of her relatives at Belle Reve either, nor they with one another, as the DuBois men gradually exchanged the land for their "epic fornications" and the women dared not admit they had ever heard of death.

The evidence in the present for this conclusion is her relationship with Stella—hardly what could be called one of confidence and intimacy, despite the genuine feeling the sisters have for each other. As Blanche dreams airily in act 1 of Shep Huntleigh's block-long Cadillac convertible and a shop for *both* of them, Stella straightens up her apartment matter of factly and responds to her sister practically, if lightly, even disinterestedly. When Blanche cries out in desperation that she has left only "sixty-five measly cents in coin of the realm," Stella answers this veiled plea for rescue from a life bereft of warmth and affection with little more than an offer of five dollars and a Bromo and the suggestion that she "just let things go, at least for a—while." Stella, out of an overwhelming desire to negate her past and Blanche with it, or out of sheer self-indulgence, will, *can*, concern herself with nothing but the mindless and easy, sensuous pursuit of day-to-day living. When Blanche opens up to her in act 2 and speaks of "soft people" and "fading," Stella can only reject what she calls morbidity and offer her sister a Coke, even as she offered to pour the drinks in act 1, scene 1. And when at the end of act 3, scene 1, Blanche wants to know what has happened, Stella is unable to confront her with what Stanley has reported, even as Blanche herself was unable to confront Allan with what she had discovered until it was too late. In a stunning unmasking of character toward the end of the same scene, Stella reacts to Stanley's purchase of the bus ticket with, "In the first place, Blanche wouldn't go on a bus." She objects to the *means* of transportation instead of expressing immediate incredulity, outrage and dismay at the *idea* of sending her sister away.

Blanche is closer to tragic heroine than many would like to think, then, "in [her] refusal to shirk a responsibility that the conventional society of her time and place would have eagerly excused . . . ," to quote Leonard Berkman. She refuses from the beginning to forgive herself for denying Allan the compassion that would have saved and perhaps changed him, or at any rate made his burden easier to bear. She struggles at the end in his memory to achieve intimacy with Mitch—the only true intimacy within her grasp—which alone can restore her to grace through its inherent linking of sex with compassion. It is thus not arbitrarily or gratuitously, or simply out of her own pure job, that Williams has Blanche declare, "Sometimes—there's God—so quickly!" at the end of act 2, scene 2. Rather, he has her so reenter a state of grace as a direct result of the embrace and kiss she exchanges with Mitch, of their recognition, finally, of a real need and desire for one another. In this light, the "intimacies with strangers," the sex *without* compassion, she turned to after her husband's suicide come to appear less the free-standing acts of a nymphomaniac than those of a woman trying to find momentary relief or "protection" without having deeply personal demands placed on her. Blanche sought to "fill [her] empty heart" at the same time that she reaffirmed a sexuality lost on Allan's attraction to men and "denied" the death of so many of her relatives. As Stanley himself says, "They [the 'strangers'] got wised up after two or three dates with her and then they quit, and she goes on to another, the same old line, same old act, same old hooey!" This suggests that these "strangers," in "wising up" to Blanche's thinly disguised cries for help and devotion as well as to the artifice and affectation of her ways, were as much to blame for her panic-driven promiscuity as she herself was.

—Bert Cardullo, "Drama of Intimacy and Tragedy of Incomprehension: *A Streetcar Named Desire* Reconsidered," *Tennessee Williams: A Tribute*, ed. Jac Tharpe (Jackson: University Press of Mississippi, 1977). Reprinted in *Tennessee Williams's A Streetcar Named Desire*, ed. Harold Bloom (New York: Chelsea House, 1988): 81–83.

[In this excerpt Leonard Quirino examines the ways in
which the conflict of flesh and spirit subsumes all other
conflicts in the play.]

While Stella and even Stanley would not, by any theological standards, be considered devoid of a soul, Williams prefers to dramatize the soulfulness of Blanche at their expense because he conceives
of the soul not in dogmatically theological but in ideal terms. For
Williams, the soul appears to be that impulse in humanity which
aspires to transcend the natural corruption and propensity to
declivity that he constantly portrays as the informing principle of
matter. Whereas he presents Stella and the earthy Stanley as the
living dead narcotized by sex, gaming and comic books, characters contentedly buried in what Strindberg in *The Ghost Sonata*
called "the dirt of life," Williams portrays Blanche as guiltily drawn
to water and baths and as claiming, preciously, that she would die
of eating an unwashed grape. The soul, for Williams in this play,
seems to be that entity which produces and is sustained by culture
but is not synonymous with it. It is that entity which, desiring the
Good, is yet powerless to attain it by reason of the inexorable
baseness of the matter that incarnates it. When Stanley, overpow-
ering Blanche at the climax of the play says, "We've had this date
with each other from the beginning," Williams is portraying what
he views as the fated culmination of the soul's struggle against the
body. The words "from the beginning"—in the mythic context of
the drama—suggest the origins of the human race itself. All of
Blanche's mothlike rushing and dashing about, which the stage
directions call for her to do, cannot save her from the flame with
which she has flirted. Though she was able to frighten Mitch away
by shouting "Fire!" she collapses when faced with this more powerful flame to which her treacherous body draws her.

The predominating conflict of flesh and spirit modifies and
includes all the other conflicts—sociological, psychological, moral,
cultural—which *A Streetcar Named Desire* presents. It would be
an oversimplification, as I have stated above, to see Belle Reve and
Elysian Fields merely as opposites when Williams has subtly
pointed out their similarity and the shortcomings they share in

fulfilling the claims of the ideal. And it would be simpleminded to call Williams's presentation of both the attractiveness and failure of these two ways of life as ambivalence and to claim that it mars the play. By pitting the sterility of Belle Reve against the fertility of Elysian Fields, the weakness of Blanche against the insensitive stolidity of Stanley, her cultural pretensions against his penis-status, her sorority-girl vision of courtship and good times against his "colored-lights" orgasms, the simulated pearls of her lies against the swinish truth of his facts, her uncontrollable epic fornications against Stanley's own, less hysterical mastery in this area of experience, Williams attempts to dramatize the inevitable succumbing of the former to the greater power of the latter. If he seems to favor Blanche, it is because she is the weaker and because, at one time, as Stella attests, she showed great potential for tenderness and trust, the qualities of a typical victim. Only her stifled potential and her futile aspirations to transcend or mitigate the harshness of actuality—to cover the naked light bulb with a paper lantern—seem to qualify her, in Williams's eyes, as a symbol of the trapped soul. Not even her moral code, "Deliberate cruelty . . . is the one unforgivable thing . . . the one thing of which I have never, never been guilty," admirable as far as it goes, qualifies her as a symbol of transcendence so much as her pitiful attempts to combat actuality do. And, ironically and tragically enough, it is her very preference for soulful illusion and for magic over actuality which paves the way for her voyage to the madhouse.

Aware of the pity and terror of Blanche's world, Williams is not blind to the same qualities in the world that abides by Stanley's "Napoleonic Code." Stella and Mitch, for example, as creatures less hard than Stanley must nevertheless abide by his rules and even his lies (such as his denial of raping Blanche) if they are to survive in his domain. Though the furies of retribution visit Blanche for her hubris in making too many impossible demands of the "broken world" of mortality, they do not seem powerful enough to affect her antagonist, Stanley. In a way, the plot of *Streetcar* is modeled on the legend of Tereus, Philomela and Procne—the rape of the visiting sister-in-law by her brother-in-law in the absence of his wife—but Blanche's sister does not cut up her baby and serve it to Stanley for dinner as Procne served her son to Tereus; instead, Stella refuses to believe the story of the rape in order to go on living with Stanley and to provide a home for their child. Nor do the gods enter and transform the triangle into a trio of birds. And, while Mitch appears to believe that Stanley raped Blanche, he is powerless to overthrow his old master sergeant whose code of morality he must continue to endure just as, in the past, he was influenced by it in his treatment of Blanche.

—Leonard Quirino, "The Cards Indicate a Voyage on *A Streetcar Named Desire*," *Tennessee Williams: A Tribute*, ed. Jac Tharpe (Jackson: University of Mississippi Press, 1977). Reprinted in *Tennessee Williams's A Streetcar Named Desire*, ed. Harold Bloom (New York: Chelsea House, 1988): 69–70.

JOHN M. RODERICK ON THE DUALITY OF THE TRAGICOMIC

[John M. Roderick teaches English at the University of Hartford. In this excerpt Roderick examines Blanche in her battle with Stanley as a heroine representing a dying, aristocratic culture.]

Had William Shakespeare written *A Streetcar Named Desire* it would no doubt head his list of "problem plays." It exhibits a curious resistance to traditional interpretation and utterly defies any insistence upon didactic statement. Reflecting a basic duality or ambiguity which renders comfortable critical statements obsolete, *Streetcar* is often labeled Tennessee Williams's *flawed* masterpiece. An appraisal of the play in the tragicomic terms Williams has set before us, therefore, is long overdue. Williams has not written a flawed tragedy in which our final judgments of hero and heroine are clouded. Rather, through intricate structural control, he has approached brilliant tragicomedy. To commit ourselves solidly to a tragic interpretation would be to do Williams a serious disservice and to deny him that element central to the creative arts—control.

With the tragic implications of so many events in *Streetcar*, one is tempted simply to label the play a tragedy, if an imperfect one. What rises again and again, however, to contradict such a position is a comic spirit that continuously puts the audience off balance. Rather than viewing these comic elements as imperfections in a purely tragic mode, then, or the tragic events as weak melodramatic elements in a comic mode, our appraisal should encompass both modes and allow Williams his tragicomic stance with all of its irreconcilabilities. As Aristotle implies by mimesis, art mirrors life. And if we give credence to Eric Bentley's decree that "contrariety is at the heart of the universe" (*Life of the Drama*), we need hardly defend the playwright who illustrates this contrariety in his drama. For the playwright with the tragicomic vision, "the double mask of tragicomedy reveals the polarity of the human condition." It is the tragicomic sense of life that allows the dramatist to laugh with and through his characters and thereby "cope with the overwhelming burden of reality" (David Krause, *Sean O'Casey*).

Williams shows a basic duality at the heart of the tragicomic genre. We begin with the traditional elements of a sacred arena suddenly profaned, but in Blanche DuBois and Stanley Kowalski the complexity of this traditional conflict is compounded. Both are simultaneously attractive and unattractive. Each has elements of both the sacred and the profane. Part of this ambivalence lies in the possibility that the play lends itself to a reading on two levels, one social, the other psychological. Although the levels cannot be isolated in a strict sense, for purposes of discussion one may argue that Blanche, as the last vestige of a dying aristocratic culture, is the heroine on a social level. As heroine she represents all that is sacred within this culture—the love for language, the appreciation of art and music, the "beauty of the mind and richness of the spirit and tenderness of the heart." Stanley, on the other hand, represents the crude destroyer and profaner of this aesthetic sensibility. His violent abuse of Blanche is a destruction of a class as well. In the class struggle neither can brook a coexistence with the other. The negative implication of such a coexistence is seen in Blanche's futile pleas to her sister, "*Don't —don't hang back with the brutes!*"

In this same speech Blanche underscores the class struggle and the social tensions which lie behind much of the conflict in the play: "He acts like an animal, has an animal's habits! Eats like one, moves like one, talks like one! . . . Thousands and thousands of years have passed him right by, and there he is—Stanley Kowalski—

survivor of the Stone Age! Bearing the raw meat home from the kill in the jungle! . . . Maybe we are a long way from being made in God's image, but Stella—my sister—there has been *some* progress since then! Such things as art—as poetry and music—such kinds of new light have come into the world since then!" It is appropriately ironic that Stanley, in the best "well-made" tradition, is overhearing this entire indictment. As the nature of his adversary's position is revealed, the lines of battle are more sharply defined for Stanley.

—John M. Roderick, "From 'Tarantula Arms' to 'Della Robbia Blue': The Tennessee Williams Tragicomic Transit Authority," *Tennessee Williams: A Tribute*, ed. Jac Tharpe (Jackson: University of Mississippi Press, 1977). Reprinted in *Tennessee Williams's A Streetcar Named Desire*, ed. Harold Bloom (New York: Chelsea House, 1988): 93–94.

KAARINA KAILO ON HERMAPHRODITIC FEMININITY

[Kaarino Kailo teaches at Concordia University in Montreal. In this excerpt Kailo compares Blanche to Kore, the Greek mythological figure who clung to the "'Elysian fields' of 'innocence' and psychological virginity."]

A Streetcar Named Desire begins with Blanche DuBois's arrival in the Elysian Fields, a post-edenic New Orleans neighborhood which contrasts ironically with the mythological allusion. The very name of Blanche DuBois hints at her physically hermaphroditic state: white, virginal, untouched by the "crude otherness" of New Orleans, she is still the sleeping beauty or Snow White, waiting for a prince to rescue and ravish her. Blanche resembles the Kore of the Greek legend in her narcissistic desire to cling to the "Elysian fields" of "innocence" and psychological virginity. We can see Blanche as a Kore picking a narcissus in the Paradise of her imagination, as she is gradually seized and carried off into her psychic death-marriage. Blanche is of course past virginity and innocence and the Varsouviana leitmotif alludes to the origin and effects of Blanche's initial abduction. Like Salomé, Blanche suffers from the "hysteric's" classic dis-ease: reminiscences. It is carefully established that the young man to whom Blanche was once married shot himself while the Varsouviana played in the background. As her feelings of entrapment in the past increase, the Varsouviana's role as the sound-track of trauma and abduction becomes more prominent and audible. A distant revolver shot finally coincides with Blanche's own mental disintegration, her final loss of self and voice. Blanche's initial abduction from a pre-Oedipal paradise takes the form of a marriage where her feminine desires are thwarted by her homo-sexual husband's psychic celibacy. For both Salomé and Blanche the seeds of rape and dissociation lie dormant in their past experi-ences with men. The suicide of Blanche's husband is more than an expression of the suffering of "feminine" men. Its traumatic effects on Blanche's pastoral self bespeak the effects of symbolic homo-sexuality on women. Throughout the play Blanche remains stuck in a state of hermaphroditic femininity; what might have been her reservoir of energy, imaginative potency, creativity, solidity—her fer-tile unconscious—becomes increasingly a fragile world of make-believe, an escapist haven of theatrical fantasies, of art as mere artificiality. But Blanche is not a promiscuous, artificial faker, sham with her cheap furs and jewels as much as she is a New Woman trying to break away from the fake theatrical roles handed down to her and her sisters by the great theatrical directors of women's lives. All her attributes are perversions of a feminine potential that might have yielded fruit, had the growth not been halted by a pro-jective misogynist environment. Blanche's compulsive bathing and drinking are perverted substitutes of the Eleusinian purification rites where excess intoxication and sexual indulgence are to have a reju-venating rather than a self-destructive function. Stanley's intrusive reactions not only block Blanche's access to her femininity, but scare, traumatize the living daylight out of her.

Salomé also deals with a "hysteric," a virgin soon to be psychi-cally deflowered by a corrupt court:

> How good to see the moon! She is like a little piece of money, a little silver flower. The Moon is cold and chaste. I am sure she is a virgin. She has a virgin's beauty. Yes, she is a virgin. She has never defiled herself. She has never abandoned herself to men, like the other goddesses.

"Silver, chase, cold, money" are all appropriate attributes for Salomé as the Kore living in a state of innocence, best understood here in a non-moral meaning of "in-no-sense." The color silver, a typical symbolist attribute of the feminine moon, underlines Salomé's unadulterated identification, at this stage, with the undifferentiated feminine. But she seems to already have an intuition that as a girl, she is "money," i.e., an object of exchange between men. From a patriarchal, Freudian perspective, Blanche and Salomé are just what the men of the plays perceive them to be—masochistic, narcissistic, perverted and promiscuous—i.e., lacking in superego and the capacity for sublimation, vain and self-absorbed—i.e., born if not inborn lunatics. From the matriarchal myth's angle, Blanche and Salomé become deviants and lunatics because they have been literally led astray, diverted from their proper path (se-ducare does, after all, mean "lead aside"). They are lured into Self-alienating theatrical roles. However, to idealize women as mere victims is to keep them in the position of helplessness and dependence. To consider the plays from Persephone's rather than Kore's perspective is then not to let the intrusive Kowalskis or Herods off the hook but to discuss why Blanche and Salomé allow themselves to become hooks for male projections.

While searching for Kore, Demeter nurtures the son of Metaneira, trying to make him immortal. The attempt is aborted because of Metaneira's mistrust of the divine nursemaid. To nurture another's son is an apt image for women's need to nurture their "masculine" potential without the incestuous intensity implied by smothering mother-son relationships. Metaneira stands for all the fears and mistrust that prevent women from nurturing their psychic integrity—androgyny. None of Blanche's "magic wands" (the Rhinestone tiara, the clothes, the masks) protect her from her internal and external enemies. Past and present collide dramatically in the unconscious associations that bring together Blanche's two abductors—the Polish Varsouviana and the Polish Stanley and which represent the beginning and end of her past and future potential. Blanche projects on Stanley the very attributes she would need to in order to protect her "belle [sic] rêve"—assertiveness, inner conviction and outer confidence. The projection brings out Stanley's need to bully what is his own underdeveloped femininity or otherness. The Dionysian energies, "feminine" fantasies constellate the outraged anima in the obsessively realistic hierophant. In a way, psychologically Blanche is willing to be sacrificed; Stanley is willing to be the brutal sacrificer. Together they are one. Unconsciously, at opposite ends of the spectrum of lunacy, they constellate the wound and the sword. As long as Stanley is a "rapist" in Blanche's mind, her unexpressed but subtle violence mirrors his. We might say that Blanche suffers from an unconscious, perverted attraction to her demon lover. Such women have a defensive, compensatory and inflated view of the imaginal feminine, living out fantasies to fill the gap left by the attributes society does not let them articulate consciously.

—Kaarina Kailo, "Blanche DuBois and Salomé as New Women, Old Lunatics in Modern Drama," *Madness in Drama* (New York: Cambridge University Press, 1993): 122–124.

GEORGE TOLES ON BLANCHE AS WILLIAMS'S EMISSARY OF THE IMAGINATION

[George Toles is Professor of Film Studies at the University of Manitoba. In this excerpt Toles examines Blanche's eloquence as a sign of the intuitive knowledge she gains through imagination, and as proof that this knowledge cannot be communicated.]

The ending of *Streetcar* attempts to recover Blanche's value through the total isolation of her voice from the somehow untenable community that requires her elimination. Williams deprives Blanche, however, of one crucial advantage that similarly scapegoated romantic outsiders in literature traditionally possess: a lingering awareness of what their rejected positions are truly worth. Blanche has largely internalized the language of her oppressors. She fears not only their persecution but also their authoritative judgment, as though they may have correctly divined that her entire means of revealing herself to others is fraudulent. When she flees back into the bedroom after seeing the doctor and matron for the first time, Stanley comes after her with the odd demand that she provide a "ladylike" excuse for her panic. He asks her if she's forgotten something, and she seizes upon this explanation of her behavior as though it would make her more creditable in the eyes of the assembled group. ("Yes, Yes, I forgot something.") As she continues to resist the efforts of the matron to lead her outside, Stanley intervenes again, proposing that what she has forgotten is the paper lantern she had used to cover the bare light bulb in her room. Other-wise, "you left nothing here." He brusquely tears the lantern off the bulb and Blanche "cries out as if the lantern were herself." It is not the light of available reality that Blanche, here or ever, declares her affinity with, but the worthless wrapping used to conceal it.

Stanley's casually violent gesture recalls the rape and, less malev-olently, repeats the realist's inalterable lesson: those who live entirely in dreams will perish. He shows her, however harshly, the difference between alluring shadows and stubborn actualities. The torn lantern in Stanley's outreached hand is his final, wordless verdict on what her "inventions," obfuscations," and "magic" amount to. And Blanche, at this juncture, has no conviction that the sharply exposed illusion (one last attempt to undeceive the dreamer) can be con-ceived otherwise. She does not know how to reassert the value of enchantment, or even to see it as a value worth restoring. In an earlier confrontation between Blanche and Stanley (immediately preceding the rape) Blanche attempts to name certain qualities in herself that might be worthy of respect.

> But beauty of the mind and richness of the spirit and tenderness of the heart—and I have all of those things—aren't taken away, but grow! Increase with the years! How strange that I should be called a destitute woman! When I have all of these treasures locked in my heart.

The painful irony of this effort at self-definition is that Blanche her-self, yet again, barely recognizes what is exemplary, distinctive, or valid about her spiritual possessions. Stanley, of course, believes that what she refers to is part of her "act" as a refined and virtuous lady. He sees her posture of delicate softness as a strained, neurotic attempt to evade the force of her own appetites, her capacity for aggression, and the meaning, for good or ill, of her troubled history. She uses her tricks of language, in his view, to establish false conditions for her acceptance as a woman continually in quest of "ideals."

Blanche's sad eloquence about attainments for which there is no reliable public measure or demonstrable proof is riven with doubt even before she is challenged. One feels she cancels her declaration of private faith in the act of uttering it, and immediately follows it with a pitiful, transparent lie about Mitch's repentant return and pleas for forgiveness. It is a brave esthetic decision for Williams to have Blanche most unerring in her appraisal of her own inner powers at precisely the moment she is least equipped to draw on them or make them effectual. The skepticism that causes her to lose touch with her treasures in the act of summoning them in her own defense is paradoxically the most persuasive sign that they genuinely belong to her. In the film version of *Streetcar*, Williams gives Blanche an additional line in her last meeting with Mitch that speaks directly to the problem of Blanche's understanding of imaginative truth. Replying to Mitch's charge that she has never been "straight" with him, she says: "A line can be straight, or a road. But the heart of a human being?" Every lived encounter is a test for those present to find the mind and heart and soul of another fugitively flickering in faces, words, and actions. It is never a case of seeing all, it is a case of seeing *more*, and to that end one strives to loosen what is securely fixed in one's own manner of perceiving enough to catch glimpses of whatever is there, struggling to be made clear.

Blanche is as careless and damaging in her words and judgments as the other characters in the play, but she is still, for Williams, the imagination's chosen emissary and prophet. From the outset, she inhabits a language so resilient and expressive that it transfigures her demeaning situation into something estimable, something allied to beauty. As the play progresses, her imagination moves, by slow degrees, further outward (chiefly in her relationship with Mitch), making itself increasingly vulnerable to the force of another's loneliness and his starved, blundering quest for love. Blanche also reopens herself to the terrors of her own past and begins to shed what is false in her gentility (the part that Stanley calls "airs"), which has made so much of her conduct deviously self-serving. She embodies the creative imagination in both its blind and clairvoyant states. At times it seems to disconnect her from everything, hiding her from the light, as it were, and aspiring to a realm that seems stiflingly enclosed and remote. Equally often, however, it furnishes a flame to see things by that is stronger, more searching than the natural light claimed by others. Williams conceives the imagination's approach to higher knowledge as painfully intermittent. Like a figure in Christian allegory, imagination threatens to be destroyed by the illusions that encircle it the closer it gets to truth. And often what it most deeply intuits proves least communicable.

—George Toles, "Blanche DuBois and the Kindness of Endings," *Raritan* 14, no. 4 (Spring 1995): 131–133.

[Jacqueline O'Connor is assistant professor of English at
Stephen F. Austin State University where she teaches drama,
American literature, and composition. She has published
articles on David Rabe, Anna Cora Mowatt, and Tennessee
Williams. In this excerpt Jacqueline O'Connor discusses
how the play's set constructs the sense of both physical
and psychological confinement.]

Although the set for *A Streetcar Named Desire* is somewhat more
expansive, with both an interior and exterior playing space, the
Kowalski apartment consists of only two rooms and a bath.
Showing Blanche inside at the opening of the play, Eunice contrasts
the small apartment to the "home-place" Blanche has come from,
a "great big place with white columns." Blanche reacts to the apartment's size when Stella explains that it is too small to require a
maid, "What? *Two* rooms, did you say?" Stella tells Stanley: "She
wasn't expecting to find us in such a small place." Blanche sleeps
in the kitchen/living room, with no door between it and the other
room. She comments on the situation to Stella, worried about the
decency of it, but what she does not mention is the lack of privacy. Her only opportunity for privacy is when she is locked in the
bathroom, an even smaller enclosed space.

Blanche's move to the apartment is the latest in a series of relo-
cations, each one to a smaller and less private space. We learn
from the exposition that after she lost Belle Reve, she moved to the
Flamingo Hotel; she calls it the "Tarantula Arms," a place where,
she confesses to Mitch, "I brought my victims." Here Blanche is the
captor, bringing men to her constricting web of desire, but her need
to snare sexual companions leads to her own capture and ruin. The
hotel room offers little privacy, for her behavior attracts the attention of the management, who evict her. Nonetheless, before she
arrives in New Orleans, she still has a place of her own. In Elysian
Fields this opportunity for solitude is gone. Blanche feels this lack
keenly, speaking of what she wishes for on her imagined trip with
Shep Huntleigh: "When I think of how divine it is going to be to
have such a thing as privacy once more—I could weep with joy!"
Removed to the institution at the conclusion of the play, however,

any chance of solitude evaporates. Her arrival at the Kowalski apartment, with a protest that "there's no door between the two rooms" foreshadows her final loss of privacy. The tiny and crowded Kowalski apartment is both way station and preparation for this final, confined space.

—Jacqueline O'Connor, *Dramatizing Dementia: Madness in the Plays of Tennessee Williams,*" (Bowling Green, OH: Bowling Green State University Popular Press, 1997): 21.

Works by Tennessee Williams

Battle of Angels. 1945.

The Glass Menagerie. 1945.

27 Wagons Full of Cotton and Other One-Act Plays. 1946.

A Streetcar Named Desire. 1947.

You Touched Me! 1947.

American Blues: Five Short Plays. 1948.

One Arm and Other Stories. 1948.

Summer and Smoke. 1948.

The Roman Spring of Mrs. Stone (novel). 1950.

I Rise in Flame, Cried the Phoenix. 1951.

The Rose Tattoo. 1951.

Camino Real. 1953.

Hard Candy: A Book of Stories (short story collection). 1954.

Cat on a Hot Tin Roof. 1955.

Baby Doll. 1956.

In the Winter of Cities. 1956.

Orpheus Descending. 1958.

Orpheus Descending with Battle of Angels. 1958.

Suddenly Last Summer. 1958.

Garden District. 1959.

Sweet Bird of Youth. 1959.

Period of Adjustment. 1960.

The Night of the Iguana. 1961.

The Milk Train Doesn't Stop Here Anymore. 1963.

Eccentricities of a Nightingale and Summer and Smoke. 1964.

Grand. 1964.

The Knightly Quest: A Novella and Four Short Stories. 1966.

Kingdom of Earth. 1967.

Two-Character Play. 1969.

Dragon Country. 1970.

Small Craft Warnings. 1973.

Out Cry. 1973.

Eight Mortal Ladies Possessed (short story collection). 1974.

Memoirs. 1975.

Moise and the World of Reason. 1975.

Androgyne, Mon Amour. 1977.

Where I Live: Selected Essays. 1978.

A Lovely Sunday for Creve Coeur. 1980.

Vieux Carre. 1980.

Clothes for a Summer Hotel: A Ghost Play. 1981.

Works about
Tennessee Williams

Adler, Thomas P. *A Streetcar Named Desire: The Moth and the Lantern.* Boston: Twayne, 1990.

Atkinson, Brooks. "Garden District." *New York Times,* January 19, 1958.

Barksdale, Richard K. "Social Background in the Plays of Miller and Williams," *CLA Journal* 6 (1963): 161–169.

Barnett, Lincoln. "Tennessee Williams." *Life* (February 16, 1948): 113–127.

Berlin, Normand. "Complimentarity in *A Streetcar Named Desire.*" *Tennessee Williams: A Tribute.* Ed. Jac L. Tharpe. Jackson: University Press of Mississippi, 1977.

Bloom, Harold, ed. *Tennessee Williams.* New York: Chelsea House, 1988.

———, ed. *Tennessee Williams's A Streetcar Named Desire.* New York: Chelsea House, 1988.

———, ed. *Tennessee Williams's The Glass Menagerie.* New York: Chelsea House, 1988.

Bluefarb, Sam. "*The Glass Menagerie:* Three Visions of Time." *College English* 24 (1963): 513–518.

Boxhill, Roger. *Tennessee Williams.* New York: St. Martin's Press, 1987.

Brandt, George. "Cinematic Structure in the Works of Tennessee Williams." *American Theatre.* Ed. J. R. Brown and B. Harris. London: Edward Arnold, 1967: 163–187.

Broussard, Louis. *American Drama: Contemporary Allegory from Eugene O'Neill to Tennessee Williams.* Norman: University of Oklahoma Press, 1962.

Cate, Hollis, and Delma E. Presley. "Beyond Stereotype: Ambiguity in Amanda Wingfield." *Notes on Mississippi Writers* 3 (1971): 91–100.

Cluck, Nancy A. "Showing and Telling: Narrators in the Drama of Tennessee Williams." *American Literature* 51 (1979): 84–93.

Clurman, Harold. "Review of *A Streetcar Named Desire.*" *Lies Like Truth.* New York: Macmillan, 1958: 72–80.

Cohn, Ruby. *Dialogue in American Drama*. Bloomington: Indiana University Press, 1971.

———. "Late Tennessee Williams." *Modern Drama* 27, no. 1 (1984): 336–344.

———. "Tribute to Wives." *The Tennessee Williams Review* 4, no. 1 (1983): 12–17.

Corrigan, Mary Ann. "Memory, Dream and Myth in the Plays of Tennessee Williams." *Renascence* 28 (1976): 155–167.

Da Ponte, Durant. "Williams' Feminine Characters." *Tennessee Studies in Literature* 10 (1965): 7–26.

Davis, Joseph K. "Landscape of the Dislocated Mind in Williams' *The Glass Menagerie*." *Tennessee Williams: A Tribute*. Ed. Jac L. Tharpe. Jackson: University Press of Mississippi, 1977: 192–206.

Devlin, Albert J. *Conversations with Tennessee Williams*. Jackson: University Press of Mississippi, 1986.

Donahue, Francis. *The Dramatic World of Tennessee Williams*. New York: Frederick Ungar, 1964.

Falk, Signi. *Tennessee Williams*. New Haven: College and University Press, 1961.

Fedder, Norman J. *The Influence of D. H. Lawrence on Tennessee Williams*. The Hague, Netherlands: Mouton, 1966.

Ganz, Arthur. "The Desperate Morality of Tennessee Williams." *American Scholar* 21 (1962): 278–294.

Gassner, John. "Tennessee Williams: Dramatist of Frustration." *College English* 10 (1948): 1–7.

Griffin, Alice. *Understanding Tennessee Williams*. Columbia: University of South Carolina Press, 1995.

Harwood, Britten J. "Tragedy as Habit: *A Streetcar Named Desire*." *Tennessee Williams: A Tribute*. Ed. Jac L. Tharpe. Jackson: University Press of Mississippi, 1977.

Hayman, Ronald. *Tennessee Williams: Everyone Else is an Audience*. New Haven, CT: Yale University Press, 1993.

Heilman, Robert. "Tennessee Williams: Approach to Tragedy." *Southern Review* 1 (1965): 770–790.

Hirsch, Foster. *A Portrait of the Artist: The Plays of Tennessee Williams.* Port Washington, NY: Kennikat Press, 1978.

Hughes, Catharine R. *Tennessee Williams: A Biography.* Englewood Cliffs, NJ: Prentice-Hall, 1978.

Hurley, Paul J. "*Suddenly Last Summer* as Morality Play." *Modern Drama* 8 (February 1966): 393–402.

———. "Tennessee Williams: The Playwright as Social Critic." *The Theatre Annual* 21 (1964): 40–56.

Hurrell, John D., ed. *Two Modern American Tragedies: Reviews and Criticism of* Death of a Salesman *and* A Streetcar Named Desire. New York: Scribner's, 1961.

Jackson, Esther Merle. *The Broken World of Tennessee Williams.* Madison: University of Wisconsin Press, 1965.

Jones, Robert Emmett. "Tennessee Williams' Early Heroines." *Modern Drama* 2 (1959): 211–219.

Kataria, Gulshan Rai. *The Faces of Eve: A Study of Tennessee Williams's Heroines.* New Delhi: Sterling Publishers Private Limited, 1992.

Kazan, Elia. "Notebook for *A Streetcar Named Desire.*" *Directors on Directing.* Eds. Toby Cole and Helen Krich Chinoy. New York: Bobbs-Merrill, 1963.

Kernan, Alvin B. "Truth and Dramatic Mode in the Modern Theatre: Chekhov, Pirandello, and Williams." *Modern Drama* 1 (September 1958): 101–114.

Kolin, Philip C., ed. *Confronting Tennessee Williams's* A Streetcar Named Desire: *Essays in Critical Pluralism.* Westport, CT: Greenwood Press, 1993.

Krutch, Joseph Wood. *Modernism in Modern Drama.* Ithaca: Cornell University Press, 1953.

Law, Richard A. "*A Streetcar Named Desire* as Melodrama." *English Record* 14 (1966): 2–8.

Lees, Daniel E. "*The Glass Menagerie:* A Black Cinderella." *Unisa English Studies* 11 (1973): 30–34.

Leverich, Lyle. *Tom: The Unknown Tennessee Williams.* New York: Crown, 1995.

Maxwell, Gilbert. *Tennessee Williams and Friends.* Cleveland: World, 1965.

McCarthy, Mary. "A Streetcar Called Success." *Sights and Spectacles 1937-1956.* New York: Farrar, Straus & Cudahy, 1956: 131–135.

———. "Oh, Sweet Mystery of Life." *Partisan Review* 15 (1948): 357–360.

McGlinn, Jeanne M. "Tennessee Williams' Women: Illusion and Reality, Sexuality and Love." *Tennessee Williams: A Tribute.* Ed. Jac L. Tharpe. Jackson: University Press of Mississippi, 1977: 510–524.

Miller, Jordan Y., ed. *Twentieth Century Interpretations of A* Streetcar Named Desire: *A Collection of Critical Essays.* Englewood Cliffs, NJ: Prentice-Hall, 1971.

Murphy, Brenda. *Tennessee Williams and Elia Kazan: A Collaboration in the Theatre.* New York: Cambridge University Press, 1992.

Nelson, Benjamin. *Tennessee Williams: The Man and His Work.* New York: Oblensky, 1961.

O'Connor, Jacqueline. *Dramatizing Dementia: Madness in the Plays of Tennessee Williams.* Bowling Green, OH.: Bowling Green State University Popular Press, 1997.

Parker, Brian. "The Composition of *The Glass Menagerie:* An Argument for Complexity." *Modern Drama* 25 (1982): 409–422.

Parker, R. B. "The Circle Closed: A Psychological Reading of *The Glass Menagerie* and *The Two-Character Play.*" *Modern Drama* 28, no. 4 (1985): 517–534.

Porter, Thomas E. "The Passing of the Old South: *A Streetcar Named Desire.*" *Myth and Modern American Drama.* Detroit: Wayne State University Press, 1969: 153–176.

Presley, Delma E. *The Glass Menagerie: An American Memory.* Boston: Hall, 1990.

Scheye, Thomas E. "*The Glass Menagerie:* 'It's No Tragedy, Freckles.'" *Tennessee Williams: A Tribute.* Ed. Jac L. Tharpe. Jackson: University Press of Mississippi, 1977: 207–213.

Spoto, Donald. *The Kindness of Strangers: The Life of Tennessee Williams.* Boston: Little, Brown, 1985.

Starrow, Constantine N. "The Neurotic Heroine in Tennessee Williams." *Literature and Psychology* 5 (1955): 26–34.

Taylor, Henry. "The Dilemma of Tennessee Williams." *Masses and Mainstream* 1 (April 1948): 54.

Tharpe, Jac L., ed. *Tennessee Williams: A Tribute.* Jackson: University Press of Mississippi, 1977.

Tischler, Nancy M. *Tennessee Williams: Rebellious Puritan.* New York: Putnam, 1963.

Vidal, Gore. "Love, Love, Love." *Partisan Review* 26 (1959): 613–620.

Vlasopolos, Anca. "Authorizing History: Victimization in *A Streetcar Named Desire.*" *Feminist Rereadings of Modern American Drama.* Ed. June Schlueter. Rutherford: Fairleigh Dickinson University Press, 1989: 149–170.

Weales, Gerald. *Tennessee Williams.* Minneapolis: University of Minnesota Press, 1974.

Williams, Dakin, and Shepherd Mead. *Tennessee Williams: An Intimate Biography.* New York: Arbor House, 1983.

Williams, Edwina Dakin, as told to Lucy Freeman. *Remember Me to Tom.* New York: Putnam, 1963.

Williams, Tennessee. *Memoirs.* Garden City, NY: Doubleday, 1975.

———. "On a Streetcar Named Success." *Where I Live: Selected Essays.* New York: New Directions, 1978.

———. *Orpheus of the American Stage: A Film* (videorecording). Princeton, NJ: Films for the Humanities & Sciences, 1995.

———. *Five O'Clock Angel: Letters of Tennessee to Maria St. Just (1948–1982),* New York: Knopf, 1990.

Windham, Donald. *Lost Friendships: A Memoir of Truman Capote, Tennessee Williams, and Others.* New York: Morrow, 1987.

Yacowar, Maurice. *Tennessee Williams and Film.* New York: Ungar, 1977.

Index of
Themes and Ideas

DuBois as tragic heroine in, 78–79, 89–91; Blanche DuBois in, 9, 10, 17, 18, 21, 25, 40, 41, 52, 69, 70–71, 72, 73, 75–77, 78–84, 85, 87, 88, 89–91, 92, 93, 94–103; Blanche DuBois's bathing in, 84, 85–86, 97; Blanche DuBois's hermaphroditic femininity in, 96–99; exile homosexual in, 79–80; flesh *vs.* spirit in, 92–94; Pablo Gonzales in, 74; Allan Grey's homosexuality in, 79–80, 81, 85, 89–90, 91, 97; Eunice Hubbell in, 72, 74; Steve Hubbell in, 74; Stanley Kowalski as Blanche's antiself in, 81–84, 98–99; Stanley Kowalski as symbol of sexual vitality in, 79–81; Stanley Kowalski in, 26, 32, 70, 71, 72, 73, 75, 76, 77–84, 85, 86, 87–88, 90, 91, 92, 93, 94, 95–96, 97, 98–100, 102; Stanley Kowalski's dissipation in, 77–78; Stella Kowalski in, 25, 26, 70, 71, 72, 73, 75, 76, 82, 84, 85, 86, 88, 89, 90, 92, 93–94, 95, 96, 102; Harold ("Mitch") Mitchell in, 70–72, 74, 75, 76, 78, 81, 85, 86, 91, 92, 94, 100, 101; music in, 80, 83, 84–86, 97, 98; Nietzsche and, 82–83; nurse and doctor in, 72, 74, 80; plot summary of, 70–72; social base of private drama in, 75–77; young collector in, 71, 74, 85

SUDDENLY LAST SUMMER, 12, 14–42; characters in, 16; critical views on, 9, 10, 17–42, 65; Dr. Cukrowicz in, 14–15, 16, 27–28, 36, 39, 40, 41; Sister Felicity in, 15; Catharine Holly as anti-hero in, 21, 23; Catharine Holly in, 10, 14, 15, 16, 17, 19, 20, 21, 23, 26, 27–30, 35, 36, 37–42; Catharine Holly's sanity/insanity in, 37–39; Catharine Holly's triumph of voice in, 27–30; plot summary of, 14–15; truth or illusion in, 37–42; Sebastian Venable and patron saint in, 19–21; Mrs. Violet Venable in, 14, 15, 16, 20, 26, 27–29, 36, 41–42; Sebastian Venable in, 9, 10, 14, 15, 16, 17–21, 27, 28, 29, 30–31, 33–37, 40; Sebastian Venable's homosexuality in, 17–18, 26, 30–31, 33–37

SUMMER AND SMOKE, 12, 76, 78

SWEET BIRD OF YOUTH, 12, 23, 27, 29, 65

TWO-CHARACTER PLAY, THE, 38

WILLIAMS, TENNESSEE: anti-hero and, 21–23; biography of, 11–13; Crane and, 9–10, 76, 82, 88; dramaturgical courage and, 18, 26, 79–80; Lawrence and, 50–51, 79–81; light and youth and, 58–59